KELSEY HORTON

ROBOT COCONUT TREES

BREAK THROUGH WRITER'S BLOCK,
UNLEASH YOUR CREATIVE VOICE,
AND BECOME THE WRITER
YOU ALREADY ARE

www.KelseyHorton.com

ISBN-13: 978-1522936107
ISBN-10: 1522936106

Cover Design: Damonza
Interior Formatting: Damonza
Editor: Kathleen Marusak
Author Photo Credit: Garbero Photography

for all of my sisters.

Table of Contents

Author's Note vii

Introduction xi

Part I: Blossoming 1

Part II: Hiding 39

Part III: Resurrection 81

A Prayer for Writers 133

Radiant Recommended Reading 137

Spread the Light 139

Acknowledgements 141

About the Author 143

Author's Note

THE NIGHT BEFORE I submitted this book manuscript to an editor, I still didn't have a title picked out. In fact, I had no idea what I wanted the book to be called.

I plopped myself down on a black cushion in my apartment for an emergency meditation session to determine what the book title should be. I fidgeted and squirmed, inhaled and exhaled, trying to create the mental space for the perfect title to come to me. Still nothing.

I had read too many articles about how to choose a book title—dizzying articles about clicks, keywords, being findable on search engines, and other concepts that I tried very hard to care about. Several title ideas danced in my head based on feedback from beta readers, but nothing felt quite right. Nothing felt fully… me.

Four minutes into my meditation, my mom sent me a text message. She was babysitting my twin kindergarten nephews that evening, two five-year-old clusters of energy and sunshine who had recently discovered that they love writing their own books and stories. My mom told them

I was writing a book too, and they wanted to know what my book was called.

(My nephews had never expressed interest in my book title until that moment. There is no such thing as a coincidence in this absurd and wild universe.)

I asked my mom to summarize my book to them, to tell them the book was an inspirational book for other writers, and to ask them what I should name the book. A few minutes passed, and she responded with the title they created for me:

"Robot Coconut Trees."

I smiled, sighed, and set down my phone. I liked the idea of letting my nephews pick the title, but I obviously couldn't name my book "Robot Coconut Trees." I needed something reasonable, something searchable, something like "How to Break Through Writer's Block and Be The Best Writer Possible," something that would get my writing noticed.

Right? Wasn't that how it worked?

Except I couldn't shake the image of two little kids sitting at a dining room table, unapologetically creating their own books with colorful mismatched markers, completely unaffected by self-doubt. They didn't think "Robot Coconut Trees" was an inadequate title at all. They had collaborated to get to that title. They were proud of it. They adored it, and they thought it was the perfect name for my book.

And in that moment, my nephews personified the unbridled creativity that I hope readers discover in themselves through reading this book. Without even thinking, they demonstrated the creative childhood whimsy that sparks and nurtures a vibrant writing life. They effortlessly came up with a title for me, then smiled and continued writing their own unique stories. I want them to hold onto this free-spirited sense of creativity for as long as they possibly can. They are the luminous, unbridled writers that I hope to become.

How could I have chosen any other title?

Peace, Robots, and Creativity Forever,
Kelsey

Introduction

ONE SUNNY WEEKDAY in May, I sat next to a priest at the Ralph Lauren Restaurant in downtown Chicago. I was days away from graduating from my Catholic university, and he was presenting me with an award that I didn't know existed, an award that only one person at my university received every year.

In my case, the award was for my leadership in environmental sustainability: I had majored in Environmental Studies, started a farmer's market, inspired students to recycle, and now I was about to graduate and presumably do much of the same.

I loved my environmental work with a surface-level kind of love. I loved learning about pressing social problems, and I loved the people I met along the way, but I also loved the accolades – the applause that I hunted like an approval-seeking zombie. I fell into the industry on accident and I stayed for the glory, following the trail of compliments until I didn't even know what my passions were anymore. *Did you really start that farmer's market?*

Can I interview you? What's your next green project? We can't wait to see what you come up with next!

As the priest explained the details of the award to me, I poked at my salad, moving the pine nuts around with my fork in little confused spirals. I was harboring a secret that I couldn't bear to mention in that moment:

I didn't actually want to work in sustainability anymore. I wanted to be a writer.

I had dreamed of being a writer for almost all of my life. I craved storytelling and its creative release. I wanted to get paid to inspire people, and I wanted to help others unlock the writing voice they kept buried alongside of mine because we were all too scared to begin. Despite my classes and projects and degree related to environmental sustainability, I could leave my environmental work behind in ten seconds. I wouldn't miss a thing.

But now I was about to graduate college, embark on a job search, grit my teeth in interviews and assure everyone that *Yes, of course environmental work is my passion, of course I see myself here in five years, of course this is what I want.* The emotions swirled through my body: I respected this priest so much, I felt so honored to be chosen for this award, so grateful for my college experience, yet so horrified at the inauthentic life I had created.

"Do you know why I reserved this table specifically?" he asked as our lunch came to a close. "Do you know what's special about this chair you're sitting in?"

"No, I don't," I said, glancing at the walls to see if there was a significant piece of memorabilia I hadn't noticed.

"This is the seat that Oprah always reserves when she eats here. It's Oprah's favorite chair," he said.

I froze.

"I reserved Oprah's favorite chair for you," he continued. "You've got great things ahead of you."

As I smiled and thanked him graciously for the award and the kind words, I felt my face flush with a creeping sense of dread. I wanted to throw up. I tried to gather my thoughts, but the only thoughts I could find were:

I am sitting in Oprah's favorite chair.

I am sitting in Oprah's favorite chair because I won this award. I am smiling, I am nodding, I am assuring everyone that I want to save the environment.

I am sitting in Oprah's favorite chair, and I don't even want to work in this industry.

I am sitting in Oprah's favorite chair, and I am a giant fraud.

* * *

At one point or another, you might feel called to write. Maybe, like me, you spent your childhood sleepovers writing novels with your best friend, switching between different colored pens in your five-subject notebooks. Maybe you got in trouble for taking the construction paper from the forbidden shelf in kindergarten because you urgently needed a cover for the book you were writing.

But as we get older, the world does its best to squish down that creative impulse in us. More and more, the same people who once cherished our writing passion will start asking us what we really plan on "doing with" our writing, how we would pay our bills as a writer, what that career would look like… and suddenly that childhood passion can sink into a soup of doubt and fear.

However stuck we may feel in our writing life, we are

capable of reversing our course. We can remember how it feels to treat ourselves with compassion, we can break through our creative blocks, and we can revisit what made us fall in love with writing and creative expression in the first place.

I went from feeling like a fraud in Oprah's favorite chair to starting a blog a month later—a blog that ended up changing lives, creating new opportunities for me, and developing my bravery muscles and writing voice. Through my writing, I have been able to create a big multi-faceted life where I don't have to choose between writing, sustainability, and my other passions. I'm still figuring it out. I'm still on the writing journey, taking one plodding step at a time, wondering where my words will lead, and I want other would-be writers to join in this journey with me. I want every aspiring writer to cobble together the bravery to write with the zest and soul that they are capable of.

Even still, I have a voice in my head that whispers: *So what? It's just writing. It's pens and papers and hobbies and doodling. There are bigger issues out there. It isn't the end of the world.*

But it's not just writing. It's creating bold and unique lives that we can live in, lives that reflect our talents and desires and relationships and income streams all rolled up into one. It's rejecting the impulse to confine our identities into one little box. It's honoring the primal need to express ourselves. It's giving ourselves permission to take up big holy space in the world. It's about no longer feeling like we have to run around in a frenzy and lie to everyone. The stakes are high.

When I graduated college, I realized that I had created

a disjointed life. I had grandiose dreams of becoming a famous writer, but I had never even attempted to publish my writing. I faked my interests and lied in job interviews about my long-term goals. I shoved my colorful clothes to the back of my closet, and in their place I hung baggy black business pants and brown loafers to wear to my new job at an environmental nonprofit. I was resigned to mediocrity, tinged with regret, and starting to panic that the window of opportunity for me to create an imaginative and impactful life was over.

So for many of us, it's not "just writing." It's getting honest with ourselves about where we have neglected our creative impulses. It's taking control of the lives we have created and powerfully choosing a new path when necessary. It's learning to incorporate writing into our day no matter what our job title is. It's liberation. It's acceptance. It's everything.

We are squarely in the internet age, bombarded at every moment by messages, articles, updates, comments, and opinions. This onslaught pulls us away from who we are, leaving us dizzy and dry and completely out of touch with our own voices. We are encouraged to move forward quickly. There is less and less time in our world to doodle, to write by hand, to poignantly reflect on our lives and stake our claim on our own truth.

We may struggle with the feeling that every story has already been told, that there is no reason for us to write because we can just go online and find existing stories on any topic. But the truth is that no one else on this planet has had our unique experiences. No one can share with the same flair and style that you can.

Don't you want to finally write that story?

Don't you want to know what you are capable of as a writer? Don't you want to know what your writing voice sounds like when you separate it from the fear and the fixation on making money?

Don't you want to express yourself boldly, in writing and in your life?

The world needs your unique voice, your individualized take on the world, your full expression. You have the power to pick up a pen, take a deep breath, and explore your writing abilities. I can't wait to read your work. I can't wait to see you shine.

Part I
Blossoming

You Are a Writer

Our minds are hectic with stories about who is allowed to call themselves a writer. Do we need to publish our work to officially call ourselves a writer? Do we need to walk around with a pencil behind our ear and scribble into the leather notebook that we pull out of our pocket? Do we need to earn an income from our writing? How many people and book reviewers and media outlets need to tell us we are fabulous before we can consider ourselves legitimate writers?

Is it true that Real Writers are the ones who *need* to write, who would die if they couldn't express themselves through a gigantic flow of words? Do Real Writers ever have stretches of time where their thoughts float aimlessly, void of ideas and inspiration?

The truth is astonishingly simple:

You are a writer if you say you are a writer.

You don't have to defend or explain yourself. You don't need proof. You can just declare it.

Any qualifications we try to smash into the writing process or the word "writer" are entirely made up. We can choose to believe in these limiting definitions about who gets to say they are a writer (which will only make us feel like we're not qualified to call ourselves writers)... or we can choose to believe in something else. We can believe in something more workable, more empowering, more likely to compel us to pick up a pen when we feel an idea flickering in our heart.

My friend took a comedy writing class, and the teacher began the first night of class by having everyone go around the room and introduce themselves by saying:

"Hi, I'm _____, and I'm a writer."

No questions asked, no watering it down, no shame or raised eyebrows. Just the willingness of the students to claim that they were writers before even beginning the writing class.

Because if we aren't writers, then why are we reading books and blogs and quotes about writing? Why do we think, *"Hmm, that seems like it would make an interesting story,"* when humor or disaster strike in the course of our day?

If we aren't writers right now, at what point will we alchemize into fully developed writers? When will we allow ourselves to utter that sacred word?

Will you finally call yourself a writer after you publish a bestselling novel? But how could you possibly piece together the time, the motivation, the grit, the almost-giving-up-but-prevailing-in-the-end spirit necessary to write a novel if you never thought of yourself as a writer during those holy fledgling moments?

You don't have to wait to say you are a writer. You don't have to come up with rules and qualifiers and sheepish lies; you don't have to participate in an imaginary popularity contest of who is allowed call themselves a writer. And you don't have to drop out of school, dump your wife, dye your hair purple, or quit your job to embrace the power of creative writing in your life. You can just… declare it.

If we dared to say "I am a writer" without fearing how that might be interpreted, the results could be revolutionary. We might start to recognize that our lives matter, that our words have meaning, and that our experiences are significant and rich for the sharing. We might start to gather in library basements to attend free writing classes, sharing our creative fears with other strangers who had the bravery to show up as well. We might start to think in stories, and one passing comment during our morning coffee could spark a ticker tape of poetry and imagery in our minds.

Writing moves us deeper into an understanding of the experiences that come up in this lifetime. We read and write to cling to a flickering hope that someone out there feels the same clatter of discordant emotions that we do. We toss our words out to the sea and beg for someone to identify with what we are saying and break through the isolation.

We can write for the joy and process of it, for the privilege of speaking our own language, for the jazzy purple energy that bubbles out of our pens. We can find teachers who hold us accountable and boldly cut through the first ambling words that we write. We can birth something beautiful out of our fear and, touched by the fire of a disciplined writing practice, gain a reverence for the stories and writers that came before us.

You are a writer. Congratulations. You don't need anyone's permission to say those words, you can disregard the little snarky voices in your head that ask you to explain how exactly you can call yourself a writer.

Tell those little voices to get lost. Tell them that you're too busy writing to listen to their humming, that they should maybe try again tomorrow except you will be busy tomorrow too. And the next day. And the next day.

Tell those little voices that your valiant attempts at writing are enough, just like you are enough, just like you were enough at age 7 (and 19, and 35, and 58…) but you didn't realize it yet. Tell them that scribbling in the margins is a sacred act. Tell them that you are more courageous and fascinating than they realize.

Tell them that you are a writer—a good one, a passionate one. And that writers have no time to waste.

Beginner's Mind

At one point when we were young, we knew how to stay in touch with our most vivid emotions. We sobbed when we scraped our knees on wooden playgrounds, we created vivid imagination-laden stories out of thin air, and we believed that we could be anything we could possibly want to be.

When I was five years old, I was flouncy and bouncy with a flair for the dramatic. A few times a week, my teachers gave us unstructured playtime when we could play with any of the well-worn toys arranged for us across the classroom: a dollhouse, books, stuffed animals, games, a plastic kitchen, and anything else a five-year-old could want.

Our other option was to write stories. Whenever our unstructured playtime began, I would avoid the crush of my friends running towards the dollhouse and grab some writing paper. I would wander up to a little round table, settle into my little red chair, adjust my little magenta dress, and write a book.

I wrote about fairies, I wrote about my baby sister, I wrote about the older sister I didn't have (but lied to everyone and said I had), and I wrote about elephants. I methodically laid out my sentences one by one and drew corresponding pictures with each scene on its own page.

Once we finished writing a story, we had to find a free moment to sit down with our teachers and read our story to them. When we were done sharing our story, one of our teachers would take our handwritten pages and bind them into books for us, books with laminated construction paper covers and blue plastic spiral binding. I loved holding the finished book, running my fingers over my name that was printed in crisp teacher handwriting at the bottom of the front cover, thrilled to rush home and show my creation to my parents.

We weren't allowed to touch the construction paper or decorate our own book covers, so the process to create a book was maddeningly slow. Every day the color-coordinated stack of construction paper eyed me from the shelf underneath the dollhouse, untouched, forbidden, yearning to be turned into one of my books.

One inevitable day, I had finished writing a story about the new blue minivan my parents had just bought. This minivan was amazing – it was big enough for my blossoming family, and it matched my friend's new green minivan. Every part of me needed to put this story on paper. Day by day I wrote and illustrated the story of my family's minivan, and on the final page of my book I drew a picture of my family waving from inside the minivan as we drove it off the lot.

When I finished writing my book, my teachers were nowhere to be found. I held my pages in my hands, trying to track my teachers down, hovering behind them as they ran around and dealt with the cacophony of elementary school disasters. I tried to get their attention, petulant and upset that my minivan story didn't seem important to them.

Finally, I walked up to the dollhouse where my friends were playing, eyeing the stack of multicolored construction paper underneath. I looked over my shoulders and still didn't see my teachers, so I reached in and snatched two dark blue pieces of construction paper. They matched the color of our new minivan and would be perfect as the front and back covers of my book. I didn't need my teachers to write my name on the front cover in their perfect handwriting – I could design the cover myself.

Like magic, like clockwork, like that bad luck that every child seems to have, one of my teachers suddenly appeared behind me and yanked the blue construction paper out of my hands: "You're not allowed to touch that!"

My face was hot with five-year-old shame of getting in trouble. I had to talk with both teachers after class, nodding my head and obediently promising that I would never grab the construction paper to make my own book again.

Looking back, I love that little girl who clenched her teeth and tried to make her own book cover, who paced around the classroom impatiently and risked getting into trouble in order to bring her writing into the world. I love her muted rebellion, I love that she didn't even consider whether anyone else would find her book interesting—she had a story to tell, and she wanted to launch it into the world immediately. Publishing her book was more important than any other stupid rule in that classroom.

In writing, we must be willing to have the eager boundless mind of a beginner. We must give ourselves a chance to find that place inside where we are electrified by our ideas, where we grab the forbidden construction paper and dive recklessly into our creative process.

No matter how much you say you want to write, you will find yourself unable to avoid that moment of staring at an empty sheet of paper that is waiting to be filled up with your words. And no matter where your writing takes you, no matter how many lives you change or books you write or scribbled scraps of paper you generate, you will find yourself several years from now staring at another blank page, once again faced with the task of filling it with letters. You will be a beginner once again.

Every art project starts with a shivering embryonic moment. Every creative conundrum can be transformed when we embody more openness, more sparkle, more of a five-year-old's ability to take matters into our own hands and see the world as the playground of unlimited possibilities that it is.

When was the last time you really put yourself out there? Raised your hand? Tried something that terrified you? Began without asking?

Where have you been hiding out on the sidelines?

Exercise: Life Guidance from Your Younger Self

We can find that creative, irreverent, free-spirited child inside of us and ask for their opinion whenever we want. No matter what age we are right now, no matter how distanced we feel from the daydreamers we once were, we still have access to those younger versions of ourselves. All we have to do is tune in.

We can interact with the glowing bouncy four-year-old that we once were – the child who picked flowers in the outfield when he was supposed to be playing baseball. We can chat with the easily-embarrassed ten-year-old, the confused fourteen-year-old, the blundering-yet-alive twenty-something, the daydreaming thirty-something.

Our younger selves have messages to share with us. They hover in the wings while we go about our day, waiting for us to ask them for guidance, and our lives can open up when we listen to what they have to say.

If you prefer, you can find a photo of yourself at a younger age to hold while doing this exercise. If you don't have a picture handy, just close your eyes and spend a few minutes visualizing yourself during a specific time of your life. Conjure a clear image in your head that you can work with: How old were you? What did you look like?

What were you wearing? What were your greatest hopes and fears?

Sit in a quiet place where you won't be disturbed, either in a chair or on the floor, and gently flutter your eyes closed. Take a few deep breaths to center yourself. On each inhale, feel your breath expand your belly outwards and fill up your body with air. On each exhale, feel your body becoming more relaxed.

Let your mind soften to the best of its ability. You have the rest of the day for your mind to hum and buzz and panic, and for now you can give yourself the gift of a few simple minutes. Inhale. Exhale. Notice your unrelated thoughts dancing along on the surface of your mind, detached from you, and watch each unwanted thought float away like a cloud. Inhale. Exhale. Repeat.

In your mind's eye, picture yourself face to face with the younger version of yourself. Take note of the scene that unfolds around you: Are you sitting? Are you in a room? On a beach? What are you both wearing? Marinate in the scene for a while until you feel fully connected to your younger self.

Start a conversation with your younger self by asking, "What is it that you want me to know? What do you have to teach me?"

Pause while you wait for an answer from them. Really listen to what they have to say—even if an answer doesn't come at first, even if you have to prod and lead and open the floodgates. Tune into that younger self and all of the wisdom they have to offer.

Continue the conversation until you're satisfied. When

it feels right, say goodbye to your younger self, making sure to thank them for sharing their wisdom with you.

When you're ready to end the exercise, focus again on your breath. Feel the muscles in your ribs expanding deeply with every inhale, and feel the rootedness with every exhale. Open your eyes and come back to the present moment. Write down your experiences in a journal immediately.

When I did this exercise with my thirteen-year-old self, she gave me this advice:

Stop bobbing around in other people's expectations of you, and focus on the hot pink lotus flower that glows in your heart. You are You— always, devastatingly You, and every time you try to sweep your Youness under the rug you end up ruined. You aren't broken or inadequate when your business casual has one too many sequins, when your dancing is "too expressive," when you still daydream about what's in the darkness.

Foster your empathy and intuition, even if you get burned a few times along the way. Take action faster. Don't hope that enduring something or someone for one more year will somehow bring joy to a dead situation.

And don't lament yourself and your life for being "boring" just because you now have stability. Remember that in your chaos of grief and adolescence and mental illness, you once would have given anything to have that sense of centeredness.

What did your younger self teach you? What bottled-up messages have you been holding onto all along?

Freewriting

Freewriting is a tool that helps us break through the physical and subconscious barriers that keep us from writing. In a freewriting exercise, we write for a short, pre-planned amount of time without stopping. During the time that we are freewriting, usually 5-10 minutes, we do not revisit what we have written, we do not pay attention to grammar and content and structure, and we do not get up to grab the snack or mail or phone call that we suddenly crave. And most importantly, we do not pick up our hand and stop writing.

Freewriting is the antidote to sitting at a desk and wondering what we should write about, then checking social media instead and losing that connection to our own energy and wisdom. Freewriting is a break in our ego's fixation on *doing doing go go go accomplishing finishing doing making progress.* Freewriting can be a meandering, a sparking, an unloading of details and a way of breaking through the rustiness so that a few unexpected jewels can emerge.

Freewriting exercises are simultaneously structured and loosey-goosey. They are timed and they require discipline, but the writing itself can carry you wherever it wants. When you're done, you can look through what you wrote and choose to incorporate it into a future piece of writing, or you can leave it behind. Freewriting is the first method that I prescribe to any writer who feels creatively blocked, and I freewrite as much as possible in my personal writing practice so that my ideas stay fresh.

To freewrite:

1. Set a timer for the amount of time you want to

spend freewriting. When this is concrete before you begin, your panicky ego mind has one less excuse to make you bolt from your chair. Hold yourself to the amount of time you choose – I usually freewrite for 5-10 minutes at a time, but experiment and see what works best for you. Timing is the key to freewriting because it provides the framework and structure that allow us to stay in our seats and break through.

2. Either pick a topic beforehand or decide that you are open to writing about anything—your day, your parents, the ice cream place down the street that you've never visited. Picking a topic isn't crucial, but it may be helpful if you are feeling unfocused.

3. Start the timer and write for the entire duration. Keep your hand moving and do not stop at any point. When the timer is done, you can finish your freewriting, but not before then.

"Keep your hand moving" is the cardinal rule of freewriting, the magic spark that makes it such a powerful practice. Do not break this rule. There will be plenty of moments when you don't know what to say next, when you realize just how tortuously long five minutes can feel. If you don't think you have anything more to say, just write a bunch of nonsense until your time is up. I copy down my internal dialogue when I'm freewriting just to keep my hand moving (*I am out of ideas… umm… what am I even supposed to write about… I truly don't know… like, nothing is coming to mind… and I'm not sure what to do…*) just to keep the physical side of writing going. Write *I don't know what to write* for the entire allotted time if you need to. Just keep going.

Resist the urge to write in a calculated, precise way. There is no time to stop and think during freewriting, no time to create complete sentences, no time to wonder about whether or not you should use a comma– that is the spontaneous magic of freewriting. Just go, and go quickly. By writing without taking the time to censor, judge, or really even think about our words, we can tap into our stream of untethered creative thought that lies just beneath the surface.

We may even begin to trust ourselves:

I said I was going to write for five minutes straight, and I did. Even though I wanted to stop, even though a pile of soapy sunken dishes awaits me in the kitchen sink waiting to be washed. I made this commitment and I did it.

When it comes to freewriting, I always use a pen and paper. I don't type quickly enough to freewrite effectively, and I just don't feel creative sitting in front of a computer screen – I feel like I'm clunking out an e-mail, ignoring my ancestral side that wants writing to be a full-body experience. If you usually write on a computer, try freewriting by hand a few times just to shake up your practice. But a computer works too. Ultimately, there's no need to get hung up on the medium as long as you're sticking to a timed freewriting practice that works for you.

After you freewrite, you can do whatever you want with the words you've churned out. You can read them. You can ignore them. You can let them simmer and stew in their papery notebook homes for a while and flip back to them whenever you're out of ideas. You can burn them. You can pore over every word. You can make them into an origami trophy, a testament to your writing prowess, a sculpture to put on your mantle to commemorate your willingness to begin.

Exercise: First Freewrite

Freewrite for ten minutes about a "first" in your life.

First roommate. First kiss. First memory. First time your heart was broken. First time you felt like you belonged. First detention. First anything.

Ten minutes sounds like a long time—and it is. But keep going, keep breaking through, keep writing even if your words veer off from the original topic. See where they take you, and worry about how they look later. Keep your pen on the page, and write rambling nonsense if you need to. Whatever it takes to keep the words coming. Do not stop.

Ten minutes won't kill you. Forget about grammar and style and rules and restrictions. Let yourself crack. Let yourself go like a child whose bicycle is racing down the pavement without training wheels for the first time. Let it all come oozing out.

Letting Yourself Hatch

Have you ever watched a chicken hatch out of its egg?

Go online and find a video of a chicken hatching. The hatching process is messy and chaotic, filled with uncertainty and heroics and desperate gasps for breath.

As each chick starts to hatch, the egg cracks open and a sliver of yellow fuzz becomes visible. A tiny indistinguishable bird cracks the egg a little more and stops, its heart and lungs panting for breath and the shell quivering in suspended animation.

A little more pushing, a little more cracking until the chick is almost hatched. You can see the chick's head and neck curled against the safe crevice of its egg, but it's too late for it to retreat back into the shell. When the chick emerges from the egg at last, it lies on the ground resting and chirping, a miracle covered in goop, unrecognizable as the fluffy and elegant chicken we know it will eventually become.

Our first dribbling words are like hatchlings that gnaw their way out of their eggs, desperate for a revolution. But when they finally reach the surface they are gnarled and stringy, wretching their way through egg glop. We wonder how they're ever going to become real birds. They can't fly on their own yet, they look miserable, and maybe they would have been better off staying in those eggs until they were a little more… developed. Pretty. Ready. Perfect.

We don't expect chickens to flutter out of their eggs fully formed. We don't expect babies to glide peacefully out of the womb, clean and smiling and perfect. We don't expect our children to magically know how to tie their shoes, pass a test, or tell right from wrong. And we shouldn't expect our writing to unfurl perfectly the first time either. When we get the pen moving, at first the words clatter onto the page and aren't exactly sure what to do with themselves. It takes time for the letters to get used to their new physical inky reality, and it takes time for us to squint at the lights and adjust our vision and understand where these words want to take us.

The miracle is that these words ever came out of their eggs to begin with. Eggs are warm and safe – they are the stories we keep in our hearts, the books we want to write but have never begun, the nice calm lives where we aren't scrambling until 3 AM with dirty coffee mugs next to our laptop trying to churn out one more chapter.

An egg may keep you warm, but it will never induce you to stay. Your wings will start expanding. You will want out.

As writers we also tend to be readers, and when we read published works we witness the tremendous passion and insights of our favorite writers… but we never see the author's hatching process. The blood and embryonic fluid has been long washed away by the time we lay eyes on the published language, and in a grand illusion we start to believe that the author's words came out as eloquently as we see them on the page.

Let's stop comparing our fluid-drenched hatching process to the final results of our idols. The moment we hold our writing up to the contorted light of comparison, we start to convince ourselves that our words are small and useless. The reality is that we have no idea how many times our favorite authors had to rewrite our favorite books, we have no idea how many editors bustled behind the scenes switching the words around and refining the itty-bitty details until the last possible moment. We have no idea what the original words looked like when they first hatched. All we can do is be fully present with our own writing and accept it for all that it is and is not.

By choosing to put your pen to paper, you have already told me more about yourself as a writer than any of your words could. By choosing to put words on a page, even though you know they are unpolished and not quite what you want, you are a warrior of the spirit. You show a dazzling commitment to your craft, and you show that you are not afraid to explore the imperfect places where your writing may lead.

So many people have dreams of being a writer, but they never pick up a pen. By writing in the face of that fear and hesitation, you create a new possibility for yourself. You show the highest and most nurturing part of yourself that you are here, you are beckoning, and you are showing up. You open up a spaciousness for the Universe to move through you and onto the page.

Allow yourself the honor of an awkward first draft; allow yourself the freewrites and ramblings where you begin to discover what you want to write about in the first place. Dare to suspend disbelief when you gape in horror at how awkward your first words sound. They are just catching their breath – they are priming your hand and mind to open up for the beauty that will unfold later. They are hatching.

Exercise: I could talk about…

Freewrite for five minutes on the topic: *I never get tired of talking about _____. I could talk about it over and over, every day, to whoever listened, for the rest of my life.*

Daydreaming as a Writing Tool

When I was seven years old, my best friend and I started writing novels together. Our writing partnership lasted until we were about twelve and remains one of the most beloved writing experiences of my life.

We developed characters and backstories and problems and absurd situations that added suspense to our existing stories. We checked out books from the library on how to write query letters, we learned about the publishing process, and we swapped notebooks at dance class with the understanding that we would switch back the following week. We wrote together at sleepovers, laughing and creating storylines gleaned from pre-teen advice columns. Our books were about a group of teenagers called The Sunshines, and each character was so vividly different from the others that the storytelling unfolded naturally. When we got stuck in our writing, we created new absurd plot twists that reinvigorated the stories.

And we daydreamed.

"What if she falls out the window, and her twin sister catches her underneath?" we asked each other, eating caramel popcorn and taking turns writing in glittery notebooks. "What if the family gets split up and Krystal needs to move away with her dad?"

There was no limit to the number of stories and situations we could think of because we were in the creative daydreaming flow. As adults we often find it challenging to daydream at first, but we can consciously tap back into that fun childlike creative practice when we want to feel inspired and generate ideas for our writing.

When was the last time you daydreamed? Do you even remember how?

In the realm of daydreaming, there is no room for the rational mind. Tell it to go away for now. Tell that cold, judgmental voice in your head to take a walk around the block for a few minutes. We spend the better part of our day judging and analyzing and making decisions, and right now we need some space to play without any logic.

Unfocus your eyes. Let your gaze soften into mush. Stop thinking so hard about daydreaming. Instead, just declare it: "I am going to daydream."

Smile. Dream of the past. Think of the happiest you've ever been. Think of your favorite game you played as a child. Think of a goofy moment you had with someone you love. Think with your heart, feel the colors swooshing out of your chest, let your forehead muscles relax.

Dream of the present. Dream of celebrities you admire, and wonder why you admire them. Think about the qualities you ascribe to these famous people you've never met, ponder how absurd that is, and daydream of the ways that you already demonstrate those qualities in your own life. How could you be more bold, more vulnerable, more free-spirited within the next twelve hours?

Now dream of the future. Who would you be if you were truly embodying Aliveness? What is the most beautiful gift you could contribute to your family and your legacy?

Wherever you are in your thoughts, linger in each space and resist the urge to blow through this exercise quickly. Really dive in and devote time to remain present in the feelings and imagery. If you start delving into woefulness, veer back on course. Daydreaming is a positive and youthful exercise, not an opportunity to dwell on our grocery list or regrets.

Once, I rode on a water jet in Florida with my uncle, and he purposely took a sharp turn to fling me off the back end of the jet and into the water. Life in that moment was salty and sunny, and my laughs were big and hearty and fearless. I felt alive. And now when I am in my cubicle, on the dirty train, in the throes of depression, I daydream about this memory to remember what it was like to feel so open-hearted.

Gaze soft, mind turned off, heart engaged. Your imagination might be blurry at first, but these daydreams are tiny green sprouts fighting to birth themselves through the lifeless gravel that we accumulate in our daily lives. Begin.

Be bold enough to believe that by making the commitment to practicing daydreaming, no matter how awkwardly at first, you are shaking up the gunk and preparing yourself for more. Your intention to daydream will make you feel more playful, and that lightheartedness will open up the space for writing ideas to emerge.

Ask questions. Seek answers. The more you practice daydreaming, the more natural it becomes. Like writing. Like flossing your teeth. Like participating in healthy relationships. Practice, and the results will unfold—and they will be magnificent. Daydreaming heals.

Freewrite: I remember... I remember...

Freewrite for five minutes, and start every sentence during these five minutes with the phrase "I remember." See where the writing takes you.

Here is the start of mine.

I remember running the back of my hand along the exterior adobe wall of a stranger's apartment in Santa Fe, thinking to myself: Soak in this moment. Juice it. Keep it for every holy memory that you can. Stay here forever. I remember breathing the New Mexico air, the November dryness and sunlight, as a moving metal sculpture spun in the breeze next to me.

I remember eating frozen yogurt next to the river in my northern Illinois hometown. I remember the first time my boyfriend kissed me, our breaths reeking of whiskey and our teeth clanking together on our friend's rickety porch. I remember the 5 AM phone call where I learned that my nephews were born, where I took on the role of Aunt Kelsey.

You could write about yesterday, you could write about five years ago, you could meander in time and end up startled by the memories you didn't realize you had. Just stay focused on the words "I remember." If you start going down a memory trail that you don't want to visit, remember that you can always change directions: You get to decide where your writing leads.

What do you remember?

The Power of Practice

When we exercise, we don't expect there to be an end goal. We don't expect to take a deep breath at the peak of a fitness mountaintop, serenely surveying the tree-studded view beneath us in the knowingness that we'll never have to run or lift weights again. We know that in order to reap the rewards of exercise, we need to make fitness a continual habit and priority in our lives.

The same mentality goes for reading, cleaning, meditating, and any other healthy habit: We know that these things are good for us, so we train ourselves to do them whether or not we feel like it. If we choose not to do them, that's fine too, but we don't fool ourselves into thinking we will still reap the rewards. We clearly identify the relationship between the action and the payoff.

But for some reason we tend to hold writing to an entirely different standard. We don't take action, we expect success from waiting and hoping that a brilliant gust of genius will flow through us, and then we wonder why we never feel inspired to write. We aren't diving into the practice head-on, flexing our muscles and carving out time in our day to write in those moments when we don't feel like writing.

Writing is like anything else: We can choose to make it a part of our life, or we can choose not to. And if we choose not to, we won't become stronger writers.

The best way to keep our writing juices pumping is to commit to a personal writing practice in which we write every single day. Maybe we write for 30 seconds, maybe for 2,000 words, maybe on our computers or maybe jotted down on the back of a pharmacy receipt while we are crunched next to strangers at the doctor's office. Maybe one particular day we will type something frantically on our phones, using that "Memo" function we aren't quite sure how to use.

Maybe the next day we will handwrite a birthday card for our grandma, and maybe another day we will create a blog post or facebook status that gets people thinking, that connects with readers in a shared and vulnerable way. Maybe the next day we will write the introduction to our memoir. And the next day we will forget to write at all, and that's okay too as we twist and wind our way to a consistent and joyful writing practice.

The medium doesn't matter, as long as we are actively

weaving the act of writing into our daily lives. A practice of daily writing reminds our subconscious mind that we are writers, and it wrestles the idea of being a writer out of that hopeless realm of something we would like to do "someday." We start to build the structure and discipline we need to take ourselves seriously.

I have an almost-daily writing practice, filled with ups and downs, unapologetically messy and imperfect. My writing practice involves packing my peacock-colored journal in my bag every day to make sure that I always have something to write in – whether or not I use it, I have one less excuse to resist my writing practice. Sometimes my writing practice is just a list of people I need to call, and sometimes it's a timed freewrite, an angry and impassioned-in-the-moment journal entry, or the beginnings of a blog post. If I skip a day, I skip a day. If I skip a week, I skip a week. If I'm working on a larger writing project, I ditch the journal and work on that writing project instead. And some days, I ditch the big urgent project in favor of doodling on the backs of envelopes.

Don't beat yourself up if you create a writing practice and have a hard time sticking with it every day. Guilt is toxic to our spirits and creative minds. Guilt is a one-way ticket to nowhere, a prison, a clamped-down feeling in our chests that causes us to coil inwards. The beauty of a writing practice is that once we solidify the idea that writing is part of our daily routine, we find it easier to get back on the wagon whenever we fall off. We see what life looks like when we abandon our primordial creative impulse, and we rush back to our notebooks with open arms.

Let it rip. You are a writer, so make the commitment

right now that you are going to write. Not just when you feel inspired. Not just when you have time. Not just on the condition that your words find their way into the internet or book deals or bestseller lists.

We must be willing to move forward a few inches and create some spaciousness in our writing practice so Life can swoop in and propel our writing the rest of the way. Direct your gaze off of the big dangly prize at the end and focus on the work and the life in front of you. Athletes don't just saunter onto the court, banking on nothing but inborn talent, fully capable of breaking every record. They practice and practice and take shots and miss shots and intoxicate themselves in their athletic practice so that when the time comes to shine, they shine.

Writing is no different.

You opened this book because some part of you wants to write. You crave it. You want to sink your teeth into everything that writing has to offer. Maybe the part of you that wants to write is a beautiful and terrified creature lurking behind the inner folds of your heart, poking its head out every now and then to see if it's safe to come out. By integrating a writing practice into your life, you will give that part of you the room to play and explore, to cascade through memories and ideas in a safe environment. Your self-expression will start growing wings. You will start hearing your own voice and realizing how unique of a twist you bring to the written word. Unplug your TV, turn off your internet, and do whatever you need to do to force yourself to begin.

Journaling and Free Form

I want to have the courage to write as if I'm telling stories to my friends – huddled around a bonfire, weary-eyed in a cheap student apartment, flailing my hand gestures at a coffee shop to emphasize the intricacies of the moment I'm trying to recreate. I want to scribble my hand across a page without fear of breaking the people I love, infusing my words with a soft yet vigilant conviction that this is indeed how it all unfolded, in Life's baffling complexity.

And I can't do that if I am operating on a surface level. I can't tap into the emotions I was feeling on a snowy Tuesday ten months ago on command, especially if in the present moment I am uninspired, staring at a dirty laptop screen and wondering what to write about. The patchwork of interesting stories that make up a life, the defining details of our memories, get lost in the shuffle and blurred together unless we record them.

This is why I keep a journal. In my journal, I record my thoughts. I write about how bored I am, how grateful I am, how confused I am about where I'm going with my life. I write about my interactions with strangers. I jot down the color of the sky, the notes from the sermons at my spiritual center, the insights that pop into my mind when my body is folded onto cushions in yoga class.

The difference between journaling and freewriting is that journaling consists of pure impulse and meandering, while freewriting has more structure. In a freewrite, we commit to a certain number of minutes and acknowledge a few key rules like "I will not pick my hand up off this page until the timer goes off."

In journaling, I don't use a timer to dictate how long

to write – sometimes I open my journal to jot down a sentence, to record a jarring moment, to remind myself that I am alive. Other times I write furiously in my journal about a self-defeating tendency of mine that just rose to the surface, or about my sisters, or about how grateful I am in that fleeting sacred moment. If I feel like stopping, I stop. If I run out of steam, I close the cover and continue with my life. If something throws me off-kilter in the course of the day, I clench my teeth while simultaneously trying to soothe myself, repeating internally *Journal about it later… journal about it later… journal about it later….*

Most of my public writing once started out as pages in my journal where I was meandering around with my words, not intending for anyone to read them, just exploring my stream of consciousness. The seeds of ideas that we find in our journals, once cleaned-up and expanded and clarified for readers, are the perfect starting points for new writing projects.

I love going back through my journals and exploring the many kaleidoscopic versions of myself that I have been in the past: *What was I doing on this day last year? What about ten years ago? How was I feeling? How have I changed?* I love understanding where I'm coming from, I love witnessing how jarringly certain things have changed, and I love observing that the "new" problem I complain about in my current journal is suspiciously similar to another issue that occurred before.

Journaling breaks down our stuffiness, our desire to look like we've got it all together. Journaling allows us to come to grips with the fact that we are all just bumbling around, adjusting our outfits, caught in a tizzy of stories in our head. It's our humanity. It's our poetry. Journaling allows us to be a little wild, knowing that we are sacred and safe when we write from a gut-wrenchingly honest place inside. Getting into a practice of leaning on our writing in our moments of fear is one of the greatest creative fuels we can give ourselves.

If you're feeling blocked, go to your local bookstore (yes, a brick-and-mortar one) and pick out a new journal for yourself. Consider the cost an investment. Play around with the idea of writing in it consistently and see what new creative blossoms arise from your journaling practice.

Ditch your journal if you hate it. Stick it out if you think it may lead to deeper creative understandings. Come back to it when you feel drained and uninspired and out of ideas. Your journal is just one more tool that can help you keep the creative force flowing through your writing, and you will figure out over time whether journaling helps lead you towards your larger writing goals.

You Are Supported

You are fully, entirely supported in your writing. People want to hear what you have to say. You have enough ideas to keep you inspired for the rest of your time here on Planet Earth, and every time you start to run out, all you have to do is ask for more ideas and they will come. Everyone you know genuinely wants you to succeed, and strangers will pop out of the woodwork clamoring to help you. If you want to write a book, you can. If you want to publish a book, people will say yes, the masses will buy it, you will receive compliments and smiles and "I sooo needed that today" testimonials.

You will start to share your writing – slowly, shyly, but with fledgling hopes that it will change someone's life. Soon after, your mom will be walking down the street in her central Illinois hometown, soybean scent imbued in the air, and a high school classmate will stop her and say, "Your daughter's writing is amazing." You are famous in your own way, and you have made major impacts on the lives of people you don't even know. You are the only reason your writing has stalled, you are the sole reason the masses haven't found you yet, but you are now unfolding and blossoming and letting those limited cooped-up feelings go. You are developing into the creative genius that you always were.

How does that feel?

We get to choose our mentality when it comes to writing. We can choose to believe that writing is hard, that no one makes a career out of it, that everyone will think our words are stupid, that we are not creative people, that our writing is bad, that the markets are overcrowded with voices and that our stories are boring anyways.

As an adult it never occurred to me that I could make a career from writing books – that little dreamy writing child inside had grown up and gotten smart to the tune of the world. I thought that "everyone knew" that authors didn't make money from their books, that every author had to have a day job no matter how beautiful their words might be.

But that's just one set of beliefs we can choose to hold onto, one rut we can nestle in to keep us safe. We can also believe hundreds of other things. We can believe that anything we write will be well-received, that people are clamoring to buy and read and crave exactly what we have to offer. We can believe that other writers are our partners and that success is possible for everyone. We can know that if a reader purchases a book in the same genre as the book we are writing, it doesn't mean that our voice is redundant—it means that reader is also interested in what we have to say. It means our words have an audience. It means we all can succeed.

By aligning ourselves with an empowered belief system, we start a creative revolution. When we feel guided, talented, and supported, we can take more risks, spend less time panicking over what people will think, and create more art. We can be true to our own voice without hemming and hawing over what "industry experts" say is possible. We can recreate the entire industry. We can set the world on fire.

The world of writing really is a wide-open field of possibilities. We can create our own rules and define our own terms of success: we can query agents, we can self-publish, we can start our own magazines and blogs and digital courses, and we can throw our hands into the air and decide that all we wanted all along was to keep our writing private and close to our chests. Some people write dozens of books and rake in royalties for the rest of their lives, some people write one book and give it away for free to support a speaking or coaching business, some people make a living from writing, some people choose to keep their day jobs, some people secure giant book deals, others will never have an agent, and so on…

Every writer deserves to feel held, like the Universe is waiting in the wings to propel our books and stories out into the world. Believe that you are supported. Trust that your words will reach every person who needs them. Dare to see whatever possibilities you are afraid to see. Recognize when you are seeing things from the mixed-up lens of your own fear-colored sunglasses. Know that the world has your back.

For Writers Who Don't Know What to Write About

Sometimes it feels like our creative well has run dry – like no matter what we try to write, the words ring hollow. Imbuing our writing practice with a sense of flexibility and compassion allows us to honor ourselves when we feel creatively drained. We can push ourselves to write consistently while at the same time acknowledging that sometimes we just need to step away from the screen and into the fullness of the gritty physical lives around us.

Your writing is allowed to ebb and flow. In these moments of disconnection, our writing and our sanity benefit when we step back and meander around in life for a little while. Drink our tea slower. Write a little less vigorously. Become more observant of the flickers of conversations that float by in our day, the electric jolts of underlying thoughts, and the memories that have made us who we are.

Despite widespread blogging advice that dictates every blogger needs to create weekly posts in order to be "successful," I go for months at a time without sharing any blog posts with the world. My website starts to look dusty, and the spam robots take it upon themselves to comment on old posts every few days, as if I need a reminder that

I'm avoiding my little heartfelt corner of the internet. But I put my blog on pause because I need to, because sometimes freewriting is all I can muster in between juggling the other disparate pieces of my life. Sometimes I write and don't want to share it. Sometimes the sacredness of a private writing practice is enough to keep my creative embers glowing.

Your writing is big but your life is bigger. If you don't feel called to write about anything right now, it may be time to dive into your life and let go of your stranglehold on your writing practice. No matter how much we love to write, it's hard to deny that basking in the aliveness of Life is more invigorating than sitting at a computer screen.

And yes, when I'm completely stuck in my writing, my words dripping in concrete clunkiness, I set my writing to the side. I laugh and drink IPAs through Ribfest, Burgerfest, and other vegetarian-averse Chicago summer street fairs. I wander through farmer's markets and cradle flavored local honey in bear-shaped containers the size of my thumb. I sit under trees and whisper prayers to my dead friends.

I sift worms at urban farms, I watch strangers dance with fire, I doubt my Life Purpose, I whisper ThankYouThankYouThankYou whenever a clock says 11:11. I sizzle in the wicked healing laughter of friends and completely let go of my daily writing practice.

A side effect of stepping more deeply into your life is that the answers to "*What should I write about?!*" emerge organically. The stories of your stuckness, your wandering, and how you emerge with words after fumbling through confusion are more interesting than any contrived topic you could come up with in their place. In daring to live your life, you will crack through the surface of your confusion and approach your writing with a fresh perspective. You will break through.

Tell us about how you Don't Know What You're Doing with Your Life, and tell it with the gusto you don't realize you have. Describe your loneliness so that its rawness is palpable, so that readers can slip themselves into your skin and begin to quaveringly sift through their own complicated lives.

Tell us about your meandering walks down jagged sidewalks, the wandering aimed to nowhere, the errands that turned into one step after another after another until you realized you had no idea how to get home. Tell us about how you handle your discomfort: the stress-eating, the stress-walking, the stress-hairpulling, the stress-spreadsheets and microplanning of your future.

Tell us about a miracle you've witnessed, even if you already hear the chatter in your head about how it isn't really a miracle, even if you can already visualize people reading your story, raising an eyebrow, and slowly backing away in the knowingness that you have finally cracked. Tell that story anyways. Shed yourself wide open.

These stories we have are real. We can scrunch our forehead and churn our brain and hope to conjure something original out of the air until we are screaming at a mirror about how stupid and useless we are, and our writing will remain blocked. Or we can let that creative light do what it wants with us, even if some days it means joyfully line dancing in a hotel basement with childhood friends instead of writing. Let your life be bolder, even if it means your writing slows down for a little while. Give your writing and your life the courageous permission to ebb and flow.

I Write Because…

Why do you write?

Why do you write when you could be doing so many other things? You could make pottery, you could lie on the couch, you could work even more hours than you already do, you could exercise, you could finally clean out that closet… but instead, you want to write. Why?

We need to get laser-focused on the "why" behind our writing. Writing is one of the first things we push to the back burner when our lives start feeling hectic, and when we have a clear reminder of our personal experience of what writing can offer us, we can lean on that reminder when we feel ourselves drifting from our writing practice. Our "Why" keeps us focused, keeps our writing on track, and keeps us rooted in the knowingness that writing adds concrete value to our lives.

When I reflected on the purpose behind my writing, the "why" behind my piles of notebooks stacked in my closet, here is what I came up with:

"On my daily and nightly train commutes, in the hazy sunrise of morning and smoggy release of city dusk, I write. I write when my eyelids sag and my head starts to nudge towards the train window in slumber, when the commuters around me stare blankly into the weary distance.

I write because sometimes I can feel the Real World's chilly tendrils grazing the curve of my neck. Putting one word next to another is my way of revolting against the greyness and complacency and regret that I see in the eyes of adults that warn me "it's all downhill from here."

I write because yesterday I saw a vanity license plate that said "PUBL1SH" and my heart broke. I write because two of my writer friends died before any of us could turn 18, and if these creative sparkles can't pump through their physical hands anymore then I need to cover more ground.

I write because people should know about the man at Union Station who does extravagant tai chi in the corner while commuters gawk at him. People should get to see his grace and silly smile like I do, should get to admire the wrinkles in his blue business suit as his muscles slowly move through space, and should get to find the peace in his unabashed individuality.

I write because my friends have already heard my exaggerated stories, but I still can't seem to stop telling them. I write because I can't sing or paint or sculpt or create any other physical things of beauty, but that doesn't dull the thud of my artist's heart.

I write because Life is too big to handle on my own, because my conscious mind does not hold all the solutions, and in this vastness I want to know and breathe and smile in the boundless unknowingness without taking myself too seriously.

I write because there is power in seeing my thoughts in front of me. I write because sometimes I wake up in the middle of the night, jaw clenched and brown eyes frozen open, sobbing with fear that there is no Divine Order.

I write because in the heat of the moment I can never find the right words to say. I write because I sometimes miss the crazed and panicked moments of losing all control, and nothing else makes me feel so wretchedly, humanly alive."

Why do you write? What anchors you to your commitment to creative writing?

Exercise: I write because…

Write your own "I Write Because" that explains the "Why" behind your writing practice. Take as long as you need to put all of your feelings onto the page, and be as specific as possible with the details.

This piece will be your treasure to revisit in moments when your passion for writing starts to falter. Know that you can always write a new "I Write because" as your writing journey evolves.

Declare It

Before I decided to begin a career in environmental sustainability, I was wholly committed to becoming a writer. A few months before I graduated high school, the mom of one of my classmates stopped me at our gigantic senior class party to ask about my future plans.

"So what are you studying at college next year?" she asked me as three adolescent heads bounced inside a moonjump behind her.

"I'm majoring in creative writing," I replied.

Her face fell, which was the reaction I had come to expect when I told adults about my writing plans. Every interaction during those last few months of high school operated like clockwork:

1. A perky adult approached me and asked what I planned to study, what my plans were, how I intended to channel my potential into the world. Sometimes they would generously take the liberty of rattling off a list of

potential careers for me: nurse (never doctor), lawyer, politician, teacher…

2. I answered their question truthfully, sharing that I wanted to be a writer.

3. A silence ensued. The once-perky adult would become stunned, confused, disappointed. *Creative writing? What on earth….* At the last moment, they made valiant last-ditch attempts to appear polite. But the damage was already done.

"Creative… writing?" this particular mom repeated, her face revealing her complete bewilderment. "What are you going to *do* with a degree in creative writing?"

I can still hear her voice ringing so clearly in my ears.

Other people are our mirrors. When the people around us raise doubts about our dreams, they are reflecting back our own doubts and fears that gnaw away at us from a deeper level of our being. These moments are an opportunity for us to see our own jarring internal critics reflected in the outer world, echoing our internal resistance. The doubts she vocalized were the same doubts that crawled beneath my 18-year-old skin. What *was* I going to do with a creative writing major? What *was* I going to write about?

Her voice was mine. Her question was mine.

"What am I going to do with a creative writing major?" I asked her, pausing for a moment to look her in the eye with teenage defiance. She nodded. Here was the moment of truth. The Answer. I teetered on the edge of offering up a dumbed-down passive answer, something along the lines of "*We'll see how it goes…*" with a qualifier about how I could always change majors if it didn't work out. *Adults always love backup plans, right?*

Instead, I took a deep breath: "I'm going to be a writer."

What more could I possibly say?

Every amazing journey begins with a defiant declaration, a statement that starts as a spark and then pulsates and grows into its own unstoppable momentum.

You already know you're a writer, so declare it. Dare the Universe to bring you what you want, and open wide to the possibility of a life where you write with reckless abandon.

Part II
Hiding

The Things That Hold Us Back

If we are daydreaming creative souls with big stories and memories to draw from, why can it feel so excruciating to pick up a pen and write down letters? What is stopping us from unleashing our holy light through the written word?

We aren't stupid. We aren't lazy. We aren't crappy writers. We aren't boring.

We are afraid.

And sometimes from this paralyzed state of fear, we hope that taking one more class, reading one more book, or watching one more video about writing will give us the skills and knowledge that we need to be successful. We spend more time acquiring chunks of writing knowledge than we do actually writing. We become experts *about* writing, we memorize famous writing quotes and keep pictures of our favorite authors above our desks and read everything we can about writing, all of which is significantly less risky than being vulnerable on the page.

We are human beings with sparks of creative light at our core, sparks that shimmer and hum inside of us as we bustle through our day-to-day lives. Everything we need is already buzzing within that internal creative light. Our job as writers is to relax the pieces of ourselves that block this light so that our stories and energy and hope can unfurl into the world through our writing. But there is no way to learn and embody this unless we actually sit down and put our words on paper.

A few months after I graduated high school and declared that I was going to be a writer, the waves of self-doubt started to hit me. I wasn't sure how I was going to cram my voice into a respectable writing medium, especially when the creative writing track at my college required several classes on Shakespeare and the classics that I had no interest in studying. The only books I read were spirituality and self-help books, but I didn't feel qual-ified to write my own self-help book as I bumbled through my first year of living on my own – enchained in codepen-dency, body image turmoil, partying, and a shaky sense of self. I continued journaling every day and documenting my experiences, but bit by bit, with no strategy to guide me, unwilling to ask questions and seek answers, afraid that my writing didn't fit into a genre, I stopped creating finished writing projects. By the end of my first few years of college, I had only written a few poems and one short story, and I had dropped my dream of becoming a writer.

I pushed my writing dreams to the side because I didn't know what else to do with them. How do you hold onto something so luminous, so full of hope, so radiant, so fragile, and so at the core of who I believed myself to be? What do you do with a dream that is encased in confusion? How do you move forward and break through? It hadn't occurred to me that I could start my own blog, publish my own book, and create opportunities for myself, so my impulses to write would rattle around unsatisfied in my heart for the next several years.

Instead, I channeled my unfulfilled yearning and passion for writing into the environmental sustainability world. I farmed kale on rooftops, gazing at the Chicago cityscape beneath me. I asked the Universe for direction and guidance, to be used as a clear channel for whatever wished to emerge from me. I met a woman who became my mentor, and together we worked to start a farmer's market in our neighborhood.

I coordinated the outreach component of my university's recycling program, I co-managed the farmer's market once we created it, and I started to question if being a writer would really make the difference in the world that I wanted to make. My creative impulse started to feel self-indulgent compared to the on-the-ground social action projects I was forming.

*What good is submitting stories to magazines when people die of starvation every day? How can we sit in a circle of desks and talk about each other's writing while we're choking out the planet with greenhouse gases? Why am I worried about pronouns and character development when I could be volunteering at a youth center down the street? (*These are questions I continue to grapple with. I have not found a gushy middle center yet, a holy place that is free from this internal conflict.)

But even as I dragged big blue recycling bins around

campus and taught students how to compost, even as I won sustainability awards, I knew at my core that I wanted to circle back to the spunky writer I once was. The creative tug was still somewhere inside of me: riddled in guilt, buried beneath the larger questions of What Should I Do With My Life, but nevertheless beating its ferocious heart and beckoning me to take notice.

Fear is the force that compels us to move our writing to the back burner when something less risky comes along. Fear is the voice in our heads that insists we have nothing important to say. Fear propelled me to turn my back on writing and pour my energy into a more reasonable career path because I was terrified to dive full-force into questions like "Where are the opportunities where I could make money from writing?" and "What does a full-time writer's day really look like?"

Fear drives us into hiding. We can chant as many positive affirmations as we want, we can fill up as many journals as we want, but unless we examine the fear-based thoughts that lurk behind the surface, those thoughts will clamor and will continue to run our writing and our lives. Only by shining a light on this fear can we begin to chisel away at the cement casing that it creates around our dreams. Only by acknowledging our own limits can we uncover the shimmering creative gold that lies underneath the sediment of our day-to-day living.

Sabotaging Ourselves

Almost every time I sit down to write, the small fearful part of me that believes in lack and limitation chatters through my brain:

There you go again – telling boring stories about yourself. No one is interested in what you have to say. You have nothing to add, this whole endeavor is narcissistic, and you don't really have the authority to write about these topics in the first place.

And so on and so forth, until it overwhelms me to the point of numbness where I stop working on my writing completely. I could recreate this negative chatter for all the other non-writing components of my life, but the point is this:

We are all powerful beings, supernovas really, that are capable of experiencing all of the bliss and miracles of the universe. We are fabulous and magnificent and worthy of our desires. We are living in an age of tremendous evolution and growth. Our cells are dancing in our bodies, keeping our skin pulled together by a force we do not consciously control. We are bombarded from all angles by things to be grateful for, and we are constantly being guided.

Yet we sabotage ourselves far more than anyone else sabotages us. We can blame whoever else we want, but when it comes down to it we have more power than anyone else in the world to crush our own dreams.

We kill our dreams by engaging in negative self-talk and by regurgitating and believing other people's stories about what is not possible.

We piss away our holy time by sitting on the internet for hours, and then we lament to anyone who will listen that we just don't have time for bringing our dreams to life, that it's just too hard to balance everything and make it work.

We let ourselves believe that success must be a struggle, that nothing good comes easily, and that we must pay our dues and prove our worth before our voices can hold value. We start to believe that we are what we do and that we are responsible for all the gaping holes of what we have not done. We tell ourselves that we're too old, too young, too hysterical, too inexperienced, or too poor to chase after our glowing dreams.

And then we pretend that we are Okay, that we really didn't want happiness all that badly, that Daily Life is a suitable alternative for the life we have been imagining. We lick our wounds by telling ourselves that no one likes their jobs anyways, that writing will always just be our little side hobby, that the odds will always be stacked against us, and that we shouldn't be so unrealistic. That we shouldn't demand a life worth living.

Stop. Just for a second.

Watch how quickly we cocoon into these thoughts and get caught in our own psychic crossfire. We sink into this toxic mess and start to believe that all of this negative chatter is true. No wonder our dreams become so paralyzed. No wonder we feel so frozen.

We abuse ourselves like this every day – in streams of criticism that lie mostly under the surface of our conscious thought, in the absurd expectations we hold ourselves to, in the moments of feeling unworthy of calling ourselves Writers. We can start to let go of this self-defeating pattern by paying attention to the moments in which we are especially hard on ourselves and our writing.

The next time you unravel into a negative conversation with yourself, allow yourself to pause and gently examine how you are harnessing your own power to bring yourself down. Notice it. Notice how easy it is to fall into this downward spiral of thoughts. Make a commitment to become keenly aware of every point in the day when you ebb into this dark pool of self-criticism.

(This is where you may be tempted to judge yourself. Remember that these negative thoughts are like wispy clouds that dance across the sky at a glittering summer picnic with your friends. We observe the shape and color of the clouds, laugh, and continue on. We don't hate the clouds for existing, and we don't curse the sky for allowing the clouds to take shape. We just point at them and let them float by.)

The critical stories that we nurse about ourselves will stand squarely between us and our writing dreams… but in a strange and beautiful outcome, writing is also an effective way of identifying these blocks and busting through them. We can forge a new world for ourselves and come to terms with the truth behind our self-sabotaging chatter, even if we only glimpse our new luminous writing confidence in flashes. We can slow down our minds and learn to watch our thoughts, exploring where each thought came from and deciding what beliefs we would like to replace them with instead.

When we are no longer afraid of our inner critical voices, when we hold them to the light and see them for what they are, we are liberated. We can move forward, even if our limiting stories continue to glom onto us, because we know they are not the truth of who we really are. We are free.

Exercise: Creating New Writer Stories

Our Writer Stories are the thoughts and declarations we have about ourselves as writers—formed or unformed, spoken or unspoken. These Writer Stories run the show from our subconscious, and when left unexamined, they can directly sabotage our creative efforts. No matter how hard we consciously try to commit to our writing, these beliefs will stare at us from beneath the glass and influence everything we put out into the world.

When left to their own devices, our Writer Stories tend towards being cramped and fearful, and they are why we never begin. They are the reason you will have the bravery to sign up for a writing class, but you melt into a puddle of self-loathing when you try to finish your first assignment. They are the reason you start writing stories but never finish them. They are the reason you have fully written book manuscripts folded into unseen files on your computer, collecting electronic dust, hidden from the eyes of every potential reader who might desperately need to hear your stories.

And no matter how many times we try to think positive writing thoughts, we will eventually hit a brick wall if we don't also shine a light on these negative Writer Stories.

Freewrite for a few minutes on every single doubt and fear you have about writing. This is no small task, but once you record a few of them you will likely find that all of your fears start to tumble out:

I'm not smart enough. No one cares what I have to say. I'm too young, too old, too jaded, too naïve. If I somehow found a way to become a successful writer, my friends would feel awkward around me. I could lose the people I love. I sound too generic, I don't have a genre, I don't know what to do, and I technically don't NEED to write in order to survive....

Write it all down. Everything. Every lingering little thought, even if it seems trivial:

My childhood best friend will discover my writing and make fun of me. Someone will sue me, I'm going to infringe on some sort of intellectual property law I didn't even know existed. I'm not very creative, my life isn't interesting, and who am I to write this stuff?

Keep going like this until you have exhausted all of your writing-related nerves. It sucks. It can be cathartic. Write it out. Keep going.

These Writer Stories don't just appear when we actively conjure them and freewrite about them. They are always dancing in the background of our minds like little fairies of doom, churning behind the scenes and sabotaging our creativity, which is why it is so imperative that we bring them to the surface through freewriting. When we see our beliefs laid out in front of us, we can see how outlandish they really are.

Once we reveal our existing Writer Stories, we need to come up with new empowering writer stories to replace them, new stories that blossom from feelings of expression and possibility and self-respect.

On a new sheet of paper, create a new empowered Writer Story that corresponds to each fear-based story you uncovered. One by one, go through each of your initial Writer Stories and counteract each one by writing a unique statement.

For example, if my first fear-based Writer Story is *I'm*

not smart enough, then my new Writer Story could be: *I am smart, I am capable, and I am always being guided to the next right action in my writing life.*

For my fear-based Writer Story of *No one cares about what I have to say*, my affirmation story could be simple: *People care about what I have to say.*

This is how affirmations are born – not as random ramblings of positive words, but as direct responses to the doubts we already have.

One by one, keep writing positive statements that correspond to each fearful Writing Story. By the end of this exercise, you will have a page (or more) of personalized affirmations, one after another, that are capable of buoying and supporting you whenever your fear-based thoughts strike.

Look back at your new page of affirmations as often as possible. Tape your page of positive statements to the wall above your desk. Sleep with it under your pillow. Do whatever you need to do to actively seek out those thoughts when you feel upset, inadequate, or overwhelmed.

Chant these affirmations to yourself when you feel ugly and afraid. They are a prescription for your individualized blend of writing stuckness, a solution that only you could have created. Let the words sink into your brain until your outside reality begins to reflect their truth.

There Is No Perfect Word

One of the most insidious forms that fear can take is perfectionism.

Perfectionism is tricky because it isn't as easily identifiable as other feelings like doubt and anxiety; it's intertwined with other self-sabotaging tendencies, and we can usually find our perfectionism linked with our inertia. Perfectionism involves setting unrealistic standards for ourselves, being terrified of failure, and doing whatever it takes to avoid criticism. Often this means refusing to write at all.

When we're stuck in our perfectionism, we divert our words onto a more vanilla track in order to keep everyone around us happy. We avoid writing about topics that are most important to us. We want the perfect words to come out, we want our writing to unfold from the pen looking like the finished products of our favorite authors... and when that inevitably doesn't happen, we spiral down into feeling like garbage. Most perfectionists either stop projects dead in their tracks or never begin.

Perfectionism inhibits our freedom, and freedom is the key we are looking for, the doorway past the doubts and uncertainties, the crack of light where our creative potential roams. To create the writing life that we desire, we need to examine how perfectionism has held us back up to this point.

My perfectionism looks like all the things I did not do, all the years I did not write, all the years that I wrote in useless hypnotizing circles that never resulted in finished products. My perfectionism looks like the day that I tried out for my college dance company. I had spent most of my childhood and adolescent years in ballet studios, but a few years before college I stopped dancing entirely.

A year into college I started daydreaming of being a dancer again. I danced up and down dormitory hallways, I pirouetted in kitchens, I swooped my toes in figure eights along dressing room floors, I secretly longed to change my career path and become a dance therapist, and eventually I decided to try out for my college's recreational dance company.

I had been out of the dance world for a few years, but I dug out my pair of worn-down ballet shoes and pulled them to my face, breathing in the smell of the stages that used to hold me. In the weeks leading up to the audition, I stretched my legs on the floor of my dorm room, sneezing into the ancient carpet, trying to edge my body closer to limber ballerina shape.

Although I had been to dozens of dance auditions in the past, the thought of dancing in front of judges and being chosen-or-not-chosen was so far out of my comfort zone at this point. I thought I would be carefree about the whole experience, I thought I would flash a big smile with the attitude of "If I make it, great! If I don't, I'm so glad I tried!"

When I arrived at the college dance studio on the morning of my audition, I underestimated the true depths of my perfectionism. The audition was a train wreck, an emotional disaster that I didn't realize I was capable of having. The teachers instructed us to perform routines across the floor, but right from the beginning it felt like my mind had been taken over by a crazed perfectionist alter-ego that I didn't know I had. I couldn't stand the look of my clunky body in the mirror, my imperfect motions, and the rustiness that left me a step behind the willowy and flowing movements of everyone else in the room. While the other girls flitted along sweetly, I couldn't stop fixating on how enormous my body looked, how ugly and awkward I felt, how idiotic I was to even dream that I was capable of dancing any longer. *I should have slept in. I should have stayed home. I'm better off just lying low and teaching people how to recycle.*

I ran out of that audition halfway through, face hot, eyes welling with juicy warm tears. I grabbed my make-shift dance bag and fled the building, back to my safe life of schoolwork and activism and wanting-to-write-but-not-writing. I had no idea how much of a perfectionist I was until that moment. I thought I had evolved into a self-loving spiritualized person, but somewhere under the surface there was a fierce and clawing and relentless perfectionist part of me.

Would you rather write something clunky and imperfect for the sheer sake of writing it? Or if you couldn't get the words to reflect your experience, if your writing refused to look exactly the way you wanted it to look, would you rather not write it at all?

Perfectionism keeps us handcuffed to the status quo of the life we are already living, and it prevents us from branching out and trying anything new. If you are avoiding writing for any reason right now, you probably have a dash of perfectionism lurking under the surface, even if you don't typically characterize yourself as a Perfectionist.

Two mantras to ward off perfectionism are:

1. There is no perfect word.

(You will write, you will edit, you will have a sublime life experience that you're not sure how to describe. You will tinker. You will agonize. You will attempt to put it into words. You will eventually share those words with a writing partner, class, friend, teacher, or stranger on the internet.

You will, months later, notice a sentence where you wished you had picked another word. You will cringe at what you wrote. Every rambling tendency you have ever had will appear in neon red when you reread your own writing, no matter how many times you pored over it, no matter how Perfect it seemed at the time.

The idea of perfection is subjective, fluid, and useless. The only way to keep up with perfection is to keep creating, keep launching, keep writing and sharing with the clearest and most beautiful words you can muster in the moment. Stay in motion. Nothing else is possible. No other measure of perfection makes sense.)

and

2. All of my words are perfect as they are.

(Whatever you wrote is the only thing you could have possibly written in that moment. Even the first draft. Even the embarrassing romance novel you wrote when you were young, when you didn't yet understand what heartbreak feels like when it sinks into the marrow of your bones. Those words had to occur for you to be the writer, human being, and expressive force of light that you are today. No other path was even possible.

Of course you can still edit these words. Perfection doesn't mean frozen in time; your words are dynamic, active, on fire. Move them around. Delete them. Mush two sentences into one. Raise an eyebrow at your adverbs. Create a new draft. But perform all of your editing in the knowingness that your words were never broken or imperfect on their own.)

Inhale. Exhale. Write these two mantras down and tape them in your notebook or at the desk where you usually write. To our rational minds the two sentences counteract one another, but together they link arms into a beautiful writing paradox that helps crash through the specter of perfectionism. Heave the boulder of perfectionism off of your shoulders just long enough to get your stories onto the page.

Guidance Ignored

A few months after my disastrous dance audition, I shuffled across my snowy college campus to meet up with my friends. I was bundled in a purple faux-fur coat and expertly avoiding the Chicago ice patches, thinking about nothing in particular.

As my boots scraped against the pavement, my thoughts in a vague daydreamy state, I heard a crystal-clear voice from nowhere ring loudly in my ears:

"Start a blog."

It felt like these words were downloaded directly into my system. I hardly knew what a blog was, I certainly didn't read any blogs on my own, and I had never had an urge to start a blog before that moment… but there I was, standing in the snow, feeling a strange conviction to create my own blog.

I kept walking, a little dazed by my intuitive experience, my mind fluttering with wonder and curiosity. *Start a blog? Why would I even write about? Who would even read it? How do I start a blog? I wonder if it costs money to start one. It could be fun… I could make it about spirituality… I could finally have a creative outlet….*

And then, the thought that would kill the idea in its tracks:

The guy I'm dating will think starting a blog is a stupid idea.

Done. That's all it took. Like a giant brick wall in my face, any thoughts of starting a blog came screeching to an immediate halt because of how I thought a guy would perceive my efforts.

How often do we do this to ourselves? We don't even start because we think we might infuriate someone, disappoint someone, or look stupid and self-righteous to the people who are merely judging from the sidelines. Our fixation on looking good sways us away from acknowledging the stories that are beckoning from within, pleading to be unleashed.

Sometimes we don't even put ourselves on the line before recoiling and assuming our ideas will be rejected by other people. I never even mentioned the idea of a blog to that guy I was dating; I simply assumed he would think it was stupid, and from that assumption I crept back into my safe little non-writing hole in the ground. For all I know, he could have been my blog's biggest fan.

I didn't date that guy for much longer, and three years later, I finally pieced together the clarity to start a blog. That blog would be my gateway into all the writing joy I have come to know.

Sometimes I wish I had started my blog on that wintery day when the impulse first caught me by surprise. I wish I had the foresight to tap into the spiritual gift I had been given, I wish I hadn't made the baffling decision to keep my holy light trapped inside. I could have had three more crucial years to find my writing voice and develop my work in front of an audience. Who knows where it would have taken me.

But I still love that fumbling version of me with all of her ideas and dreams and insecurities, who wasn't quite ready to start the blog that she wanted to write. I love her excitement and her doubting. I love her humanness. I love her flagrant disregard for her own wisdom. I love that the memory of her has sparked me to write, achieve, and expose my writing to the world.

This Universe is not a withholding universe: we can't "blow it," we can't "miss our chance" or "throw that opportunity away" or fall prey to any other slew of imaginary failure stories. If we miss the boat once, a new boat will come around again – our boat this time, the boat that is a little more perfect for us. The boat we should have taken all along.

No matter what guidance you have ignored in the past, no matter what urges you have stuffed down because they felt unsafe at the time, every moment is a new opportunity to choose again, with eyes wide open to the new miracles and ideas that are waiting for you to allow them in. There is no such thing as failure or lost opportunity.

In this moment, you are exactly where you need to be in your writing. Nothing could have brought you anywhere else. So when are you going to break free? How much guidance are you going to ignore before you finally move forward?

Freewrite: Guidance Ignored

Freewrite for ten minutes on a time in your life when you had the urge to do something, say something, or go somewhere, but you held back because you were afraid of what people would say.

Was it the play you never tried out for? The admission of love that you never made to the girl in your fourth-grade class? The words you were too bashful to say?

Let this freewrite take you into the tiny critical stories of your life that you have nearly forgotten.

The Myth of "I Don't Have Time"

One of the biggest lies we tell ourselves is "I don't have time."

We say this constantly. We say it to the fundraisers who wear neon vests and try to intersect our path on the sidewalk, sweetly requesting a charitable donation. We say it when we're frustrated with a family member's antics. We say this when we have a hazy dream inside that we're afraid to start.

Every single writing class I have taken has been riddled with people who say they "don't have time" to write, myself included. But "I Don't Have Time" is a statement that takes the responsibility off of us. When we Don't Have Time, we are the victim, the poor little wannabe writer who drew the short straw and is stuck with having to make a living and cram our writing in with the rest of our absurd and hectic lives.

When we passionately defend our position that we "don't have time" to write, all we do is keep ourselves stuck. The planet teeters onward, some people live bold luminous radiant lives, some people write books… and gosh, we would too, if only we had the Time.

But the cold truth is that we will never feel like we have enough time to write. We must fight to carve out slivers of our day to write, because someone else, someone just as busy and frantic as we are, will find a way to write a gorgeous book on the same limited amount of time as we all have. And we will be left in the dust wondering why our words are still secret, still hidden, still shifting uneasily inside us.

During my sophomore year of college, my sister found out she was pregnant with twins. She spent several months on bed rest in a suburban hospital room, hooked up to wires and monitors as two babies kicked at her insides. I tried to balance my job, my classes, my friendships, and my desire to launch a farmer's market, all while trekking two hours each way on public transit to her hospital bed as often as possible. I thought there was no way I could juggle it all.

And I didn't. Several of my friendships disintegrated during those months – those people sent me angry messages about how I wasn't hanging out with them enough, and we haven't spoken since. I used to think those relationships fell apart because I was too busy, but looking back, that wasn't the case.

During that frenzied period of my life, I still managed to spend time with the friends who were supportive and authentic and present. The ones who would never "dump" me, who loved me unconditionally, who accepted that we wouldn't see each other much, who threw me a birthday party in their studio apartment and let me sob on their fuzzy blue futon while they applied to medical school.

Time expands when we decide that certain people and experiences are a crucial part of our lives. As it turns out, I did have time for friends – much less time than before, but little slivers of space that continued to present themselves nevertheless. But because I was forced to choose how to spend that limited time, the clingy friends who demanded my constant attention were the first ones to fall away.

When it comes to our dreams, our writing, and the exquisite (and maybe undefined) things we want to accomplish in this lifetime, we have to break free of the "I Don't Have Time" trap. No one can magically make extra time appear for us. We have to make the time. And when the pain of living a drab and half-awake life becomes great enough, we can let the strength of our vision propel us onwards no matter how busy we are.

Maybe you don't think you have the time to write. Maybe your mom is sick and your car is constantly breaking down and you work crazy hours and haven't seen that one friend from childhood in so long and you feel like you *need* to squeeze him in. Maybe you're on the verge of a breakdown and your kids are ripping the batteries out of their toys in the other room and the bills are piling up and you don't know where you put your keys again.

How can we possibly get it all done?

By taking a deep breath. By trusting that we have all the time we need. By browsing the internet less and laser-pointing our energy on our real-life visions. By remembering that time expands in miraculous ways, that we are fully supported, and that our future moves steadily towards us as we move towards it. By banishing "I Don't Have Time" from our vocabulary when it comes to the pursuits we love.

The world needs your work and your light, your dreams and your projects. You have time to unleash that dazzling greatness from inside you. You have time to write. Dump the excess, the mind-numbing compulsive habits, the social media, the superficial friends, the events you say "yes" to out of obligation. Hone in on what's important. Scribble down bits of poetry in between train stops. Close your computer. Doodle in the margins. Say "No thank you" as an act of self-respect.

Let your vision pull you. Honor your sacred, holy time. Your future readers will thank you. You're on fire already.

Exercise: If I had time, I would…

Freewrite about everything you would do if you had more time. Be as specific or general as you want, but go for ten minutes to get the juices flowing and crack through the monotonous surface of our first impressions:

If I had time, I would play with my nephews, I would work out, I would write thank-you notes, I would remember to wash my face at night, I would fix my website and call my cousin, I would always have fresh new writing ideas….

Let this freewrite simmer for a few days, and then consciously go back and reread it. What themes repeat themselves? What desires are prominent throughout your freewrite? These are the yearnings that are crucial to your life's unfolding. When you have moments of wondering how to bring more joy and enthusiasm into your life– start here.

We never technically get more time, but time can feel like it expands when we become more conscious of how we use it. Declare that you're going to accomplish something from your freewrite this week, and then honor your word. Slip one tiny new habit into your week, even if it feels uncomfortable and that little scared voice inside insists that you don't have the time. Honor yourself enough to incorporate something small and new into your life as a reminder that it can be done.

Love Thyself

Making the choice to pick up a pen, tune out the world, and spend time in our own feelings is a radical act of self-love. By carving time out of our day to write, we make a commitment to ourselves that we are important and that our memories, thoughts, stories, and moods are worth acknowledging.

Many of us have been told at some point that our voice doesn't matter – that we need to quiet down, let things go, and stop being so sensitive. Many of us have been silenced because of our gender, race, sexual orientation, income, or background, again guided to believe that the world would turn more smoothly if we just kept our lips sealed. By picking up a pen and letting our feelings spill onto the page, we reclaim the luminous power of our own voice.

When we write, we remember that we are bigger than the sound bites and social media snippets that comprise our modern world. We step back from society's messages about who we should be, and we choose to rediscover who we truly are.

Do you know what your handwriting looks like? Do your letters become loopier when you are elated with life? Do your sentences shrivel up when you feel lost? Embrace these tiny and miraculous discoveries you make about yourself.

What does your writing voice sound like? You have your own writing style pulsing through you and waiting to be discovered. Writing allows us to get to know these vibrant pieces of ourselves that lie just beneath the surface.

When we first put words down, they are often cramped, clunky-sounding, and imperfect. This will always be the case, and it is okay. We are tasked with the feat of reminding ourselves over and over again that it's okay for our words to clink together oddly at first. We get to practice non-judgment in these moments as we learn to accept ourselves exactly where we are today.

You are enough. You can write in highlighter in a tattered empty notebook you found under your brother's bed. You can scribble in the margin of a receipt that you found in the bottom of your purse. You can tearfully fumble words together in ways that don't make sense in that moment. And you are still enough.

If you feel called to share your writing, we no longer need to wait for a publisher to give us permission to be artists. Start a blog. Write a love letter. Self-publish a novel. Dust off that story you wrote when you were seven, the one that lives in a green folder in the dusty corner crevice of your closet. Begin.

Writing is brave. Too many people will sit quietly on their hands, deny their own creative power, and maintain the status quo with their stories locked inside. Choose bravery instead.

Know Thyself

Do you work better in the morning, before your mind is fuzzy with current events and children and to-do lists? Or do you work better at night? Do you play music in the background when you write, or does that distract you? Do you like to hold a pen, that sacred tool of creation that has propelled our stories along for centuries, and watch your handwriting loop-de-loop into an expression of your soul? Or do you work better on a computer screen, where you can save your work and move words around freely like the intricate puzzle pieces they are?

I don't read or write much fiction. I once understood the allure of creating characters and stories through fiction, of feathering your life into pieces and hiding those pieces in scenes and dialogue. Like real life… but a little bigger, a little more controllable, a little more free. I have a healthy respect for fiction writers, but I know myself, and I know that it's not worth it for me to try to grit my teeth and force myself to write a fiction story right now. It's just not something I feel called to create.

(Leave the door open for unexpected changes in direction. At some point, when I'm stuck and lost and unsure of my voice, I may write a fiction story to jolt myself out of my comfort zone.)

But if you love fiction, if you daydream in characters and stories and plot twists, by all means write fiction. Let it rip. The passion behind your project will magnetize the inspiration and readers to come knocking at your doorstep, guided like moths to your fiery commitment to your craft. Hold onto that grace that keeps you interested in your projects, your message, and your voice.

I also don't work well typing on screens. Anything interesting that I have ever written has started with pen on paper. Then I retype those words on the screen, and from there I add to them, write more, delete some, and play around with the language. I like to create the original skeleton in my own handwriting.

Once you start understanding your ideal writing styles and conditions, try to create them as often as possible. But the flip side of knowing our preferences is that we need to be wary of using these idealized perfect conditions as a crutch or an excuse. Writing can be done in snippets of train rides, in waiting rooms, in bleachers at swim practice. If slivers of time in the evenings are the only time you have to write, then you had better get used to writing in the evenings for now. If you don't have the luxury of writing by hand because you're shoving a lumpy frozen meal into your mouth in front of your keyboard at work on your lunch break, type your stories out with as much joy and soul as you can muster. If you're taking a fiction writing class for the next six weeks, you had better learn how to pump out some fiction.

No one is going to change your life for you, and nobody is going to write your stories for you. The world will not always conform to the perfect writing conditions that you desire – peaceful, serene, sunny, bursting with creative potential. You must keep making efforts, showing up, participating in your creative journey, moving inches so that the Universe will skyrocket you forward for miles.

Victimization and excuse-making are one-way tickets to staying cemented in the same exact place you are right now. Know yourself, facilitate your own needs, be gentle with yourself (some days are just not good days to write, and that's okay), but keep consistently showing up to the page no matter what.

You Cannot Die of Writer's Block

Every time I hear someone say "I have Writer's Block," I cringe.

You may know the drill about Writer's Block: we are writing (or more likely, we are not writing) and suddenly the blank page looms before us. And we can't think of anything to write about. The words and ideas are nowhere to be found, the stories evaporate into nowhere, and any sentences that we do manage to squeeze out sound clumsy and generic. We feel like we have lost our groove, like the doorway to our usual creative flow has been sealed off by gremlins. Everything stops working.

So we declare: "I have Writer's Block."

And this moment, this moment of giving Writer's Block its own name and power, is where all the trouble begins.

Writer's Block is not a disease. It's not the flu that you caught from a drippy kid at preschool, it's not the contagion that sets our media afire with panic, and it's not the ailment that kept you out of gym class as a child. No one has ever died of Writer's Block. I have never seen swarms of people walking in matching colored T-shirts to raise money to find a cure for Writer's Block. The best scientific minds of the 21st century have yet to decide that Writer's Block is important enough to solve.

Because Writer's Block does not exist.

The term "Writer's Block" is a concept we created, and enough people talked about it that we chose to believe in it. We stared at a blank page long enough and decided the phenomenon needed its own diagnosis. Entire books exist on how to break out of Writer's Block, but still we yearn for more information, more secrets, the golden answers that will keep our writing flowing around the clock.

When we say we "have Writer's Block," all we're really saying is that we are creatively blocked. No more, no less. We, the magnificent artistic creatures who are capable of spinning interactions with strangers into long telltale stories, are feeling temporarily blocked in our creativity. We are co-creators of our creative blocks, they have their own lessons to teach us, and like with any other kind of stuckness in our lives, we are capable of finding our way back to the light again.

The reason I'm so adamant about this subject is that when we say "I have Writer's Block," we avert all responsibility from ourselves. When we stay in this space, blaming an outside force for our lack of inspiration, there is no possibility for growth and creative evolution.

When you're feeling creatively blocked, treat yourself with compassion. Take a break and do some gardening, rework your life, spend time with your family, take a different route to work—do something, anything, to shake up the pieces of your life.

My most extreme stints of being creatively blocked have occurred when I was just on the cusp of creating something amazing, but I had no idea at the time. Don't quit writing right when it gets interesting. Hold out for the miracle. Try a freewriting exercise, try stepping away and switching to another writing piece, try getting some physical exercise to stir up your energy.

I dare you to eliminate the phrase Writer's Block from your vocabulary – it will only keep you feeling sick and stuck. There are so many more alive and empowering ways that we can talk about so-called Writers Block, and of course you can come up with your own as well:

I'm feeling stuck right now in my writing. I don't feel the ideas coming to me right now. I know the words are on their way, but right now I feel disconnected. I need to change something up. I need to stop thinking and start allowing.

We suffocate our own vitality when we don't believe we're good enough. We can't write from the soul when all we hear is our own inner criticism. When we scratch beneath the surface of our Writer's Block, we can find the hazy reasons of why we aren't writing—and they are bigger than "I just don't feel like writing." They are the doubts we harbor at our core about not being worthy of expressing our voice.

Writers are conduits through which an enormous creative life force funnels into the world. When we say what we are drawn to say, we have the potential to transform the world. My prayer when I sit down to write is: *Let me write what needs to be written.* And sometimes nothing wants to emerge at first. And that is the perfect place to begin.

All we have to do is get out of the way. We need to get out of the way of the incredible friendships and forks in the road and opportunities that are trying to find us, if only we weren't so busy lamenting why nothing good ever happens to us. We need to get out of the way of the fiery and incredible love in our relationships that is pulsating beneath the surface and trying to shine through, ready to appear if only we weren't so preoccupied with being right. And we need to get out of the way of the words that want to pour forth from us, the words that would be on the page by now if only we weren't so hung up on pleasing our readers or sounding smart or protecting the truth.

Writers who aren't writing are just hiding. Lean into your one-of-a-kind writing voice, allow the words to hatch, hold your ear to the conch shell of your heart, and listen hard for the stories that hum beneath the surface of your stuckness. You are so much bigger than your so-called Writers Block, and an energy that is bigger than you wants to flow through you. Let it rip.

Writing What You Know

"Write what you know" seems like the most repeated writing advice out there. It can also come off as the most confusing and the most boring – how can we stretch and grow if we just stick to what we know? What if our lives are boring? What if the things we know don't spark us with the passion and excitement to write?

I believe in writing what we know. The problem is that we don't give ourselves credit for just how much we know and just how juicy our lives really are.

Write What You Know means we can mine our lives for content and share those stories with the world in all their messiness and flaws and grace. Our daily lives are full of richness and color. We are all brimming with stories and details that are waiting to be let out into the world, and every day we take in even more stimuli. Snippets of conversations. Dying yellow roses. A flicker of a memory of a vacation gone wrong. The occurrences and thoughts that we brush off as Normal and Boring are sacred experiences that no one else can share in quite the same way we can, and these experiences deserve to be expressed.

Write What You Know means we don't have to squish our eyebrows together and conjure up new ideas to put on paper; the details are already within us, and our job is to get our self-sabotaging thinking out of the way and let the words burst forth.

I have spent hours waiting for inspiration to strike while ignoring my inner ticker tape of dialogue that reveals my deepest passions, struggles, and revelations – the exact topics that are rich and earthy and writable. I have mistakenly looked Out There for interesting topics to write about. This kind of frantic seeking unfailingly comes up short: I blunder around in an aura of Writer's Block, doubting my gifts and ignoring the treasure trove of my own life experiences that lie just under the surface of my existence.

Just because you went to school and learned about a particular topic doesn't mean you have to write about it. You can write about your family vacations or lack of family vacations. You can write about the two birds that started flapping and gnawing at each other as you got out of your car yesterday. You can write about your tics. You can write about your friendships – the childhood ones, the nurturing ones, the ones that feel like a needy and codependent road to nowhere.

You can write these stories as poetry, as fiction, as blog posts, as memoirs. You can choose to ease off the topics themselves and write inspirational stories that vaguely refer to memories from your life. You can make your stories into whatever you want.

We take so much in, but we block ourselves from letting it out again out of self-doubt, shame, or fear that our stories aren't Interesting Enough. That we will sound stupid. That no one cares. But if you dare to let your stories out, if you allow them to expand from their cramped little boxes in your heart, they can help you see your life from a new perspective that brims with deeper meaning.

Inhale the details, the life experiences, the ideas and muses and inspiration. And then exhale it all back into the world through your stories and songs. Fill up the well, and release it off into the world again. If you feel creatively blocked, if you want to write or make art or explore your life or make better conversation, you are probably overlooking oodles of magical content.

One evening, I found myself pacing back and forth in my small damp apartment wondering what my next blog post should be about. I had a few half-written ideas but nothing seemed to be working, and I was starting to wonder if I was out of ideas for good.

A few minutes later a friend sent me a message, and since I was looking for anything to do to get out of writing, I read it immediately. He reached out to me because he was struggling with anxiety, and he was wondering what techniques I use to calm myself down when I get nervous, panicky and jittery.

I felt his anguish. I nodded in familiarity as he

described the frustration of trying different tactics and still feeling that fearful tension. I sat down and spent over an hour writing a message back to him – deleting words, reworking my explanations of the mindfulness exercises that help me, creating bulleted lists to make my ideas easier to follow. I shared a list of strategies that have helped me along the way, and I confessed that my relationship with darker emotions is something I handle every day. Every word from me was heartfelt and authentic, dripping in loving honesty because I was speaking directly to my friend. The words bubbled out one after another after another, and I felt unstoppable.

I looked over the message one last time and sent it to him. Then I went right back to pacing around my room, wondering what I could possibly write about on my blog.

Except I didn't need to think of something new to write about on my blog– I could write about my anxiety. The anxiety I had just written about for an hour, the strategies that other people with anxiety would love to hear about… all of that would be useful and authentic to my readers, but I almost missed an opportunity to share it with them because I was so preoccupied with coming up with a new idea.

Our lives and words and stories are right under our noses. Our individual stories are little representations of the human experience – you could write about any small moment and memory, and with it can come the floods of self-discovery, the seeds of universal truth that will have readers nodding their heads in awe. We take our stories for granted, but the truth is that they could be supremely useful to someone else. Let it be easy. Start your writing exactly where you are.

Exercise: Pay Attention

Our lives are overflowing with divine content that we take for granted. If you don't know what to write about, start by skimming through the themes, activities, and conversations of your own daily life.

What calls to you? What three-hour conversations do you have without realizing the clock has moved? What books are on your bookshelf? Begin there.

Have you ever grieved the loss of someone you hardly knew? Who? And why? And how did that alter your core beliefs about Life?

If someone handed you a million dollars tomorrow, what would you do with it? What does that say about you?

What pissed you off yesterday? When did you have to bite your tongue and keep quiet this week? What habits are you trying to break free from? What are you afraid of?

Pay attention to these details of your own sacred life, and you will soon find that a day in your life could birth hundreds of little stories and snippets and truths. Everything you want to write about is already hovering in front of your eyes, and when you find those stories, when you see them for what they are and share them with us, your authenticity and voice will make your writing so much stronger. We will want to cling to every word.

Fierceness and Bite

I was once involved in a writing project for someone else's blog, and the assignment was to create a "Dear Dancer" letter directed at young ballerinas.

I spent the better part of my childhood and adolescent years as a ballerina. I sauntered powerfully down jazzy grey dance floors, performed with a beaming smile onstage, sobbed in dressing rooms, and learned a few lessons along the way. This letter was not going to be about how to point your toes or tantrum your way into a starring role – it would be brimming with guidance, directed at the messily insecure adolescent dancers of today. I wanted my writing to celebrate dance while acknowledging the difficulties of watching your passion morph into something more competitive and body-image focused than you ever wanted.

I wrote long arcing sentences about how intimately dancers cradle our insecurities, how exposed we are when we're surrounded by mirrors, and how flubbery we feel on the days our bodies don't want to play along. I wrote about the day I became an assistant dance teacher and the deep joy I felt in teaching self-expression to my students. I wrote about how my love for teaching dance classes swelled up within me even as my personal desire to become a professional dancer faded into nothing.

But these big sweeping themes don't hook anybody's attention – they're just biography, broad statements that we might find in a third grade essay about what we did over the summer. I danced. It got ugly. I quit dancing. I taught dancing. I moved on. The End.

Glassy non-specific summaries are for cubicles and

Christmas parties. To tell a good story, one that rocks our readers and does justice to our exuberantly complicated life experience, we need to dive straight into the heart of the messy details.

Don't write *about* what happened. We don't want to hear *about* your childhood of growing up in a fundamentalist family, like you were talking about the weather or the latest war your country has become embroiled in. We don't want you to dance around the edges of your truth. We want to see you at age 9, 11, 17, looking up at the glint of the moon and beginning to doubt whether anyone was out there listening to you, hiding your copy of the Tao Te Ching in the sleeve of your pillowcase, running your fingers across the snag in the seat of your blue chair in the church sanctuary for the last time.

We tend to gloss over these details in daily conversation, but writing is our chance to go back and zoom in deeper, change the angle, come to new understandings and capture moments as they were. These details fade away if we don't get them down in concrete terms, and we are left with brushstrokes of fuzzy memories that lose their fierceness and bite over the years.

When we settle into these details, we momentarily let go of our mind in all of its expectations and regrets and fears of the future. We tell stories that grip people. We remember the truth of our lives, and we set the world on fire.

Sometimes the larger arc of our life is overwhelming. Sometimes we grapple with why everything unfolds the way it does. Sometimes Life or shock or depression slam against us, and in those moments it can be enough to be present to our blue-cased pen that writes in black ink, the sequined purse we bought eight weeks ago that's already falling apart, the white peach tea that the barista initially forgot to make. We center into the present moment, that elusive sacred space that is, frustratingly enough, the only moment we can control.

We will squint our eyes towards the horizon, shake off the fuzziness beneath our forehead, and find ourselves lost in memories of squeaky pale ballet shoes, a teacher's fingers prodding at our stomach flesh while telling us to do more crunches, paper maché mouse-shaped headpieces that covered our faces and kept our hot breath fogged against our skin in The Nutcracker.

And we will tell about it.

Coming Out of Hiding

I don't know what compels some of us to write. I don't know why I clawed voraciously at books and blank pages from a young age, walking through office supply stores and running my hands along the notebooks, gleefully planning out the colorful writing studio I would have When I Grew Up. It's the same divine rattling that causes us to start big sweeping projects, to look someone in the eye for the first time and know that they are going to become a very big part of our future.

So why do we hide?

That little child inside of us still wants to write. That child has vibrant and beautiful things to say to the world, observations to proclaim, stories to tell, and they have been waiting patiently for you to open up and get your hands moving. They have been waiting for you to commit a moment of your life to writing and creating work that matters.

Other people have voices, and we listen to them all the time. We zone out and scroll through social media, bombarded by the voices of others; we eat complimentary breakfast on Styrofoam plates at greying hotels, and we hear the voices on TV talking every which way about current events. None of this seems to phase us.

And if other people get to have voices, then we get to have a voice too. We are allowed to stand up, to write and raise our hands and shout out the answers and fumble through those answers the best we know how. The privilege of speaking up and shining our lives into the world isn't reserved for Someone Else – it's already ours. It has always been ours. It's up to us to claim that voice again, to remember who we are and who we are here to become.

During my final semester of college, I took my first formal creative writing class. Several of the students in my class were committed writers, the kind of people who had spent college furiously scribbling away and creating multiple book manuscripts, who had special writing software on their computer, and who had a clear future in writing. Some of the other students had never written before but had always wanted to dip their toes into the creative waters. I was huddled closer to these students, excited to take the class but afraid at the thought of writing for an audience – even if that audience was an equally-nervous ragtag group of peers chatting around a table.

Our serene and long-haired teacher asked us to go around the room and share what kind of writing we do. I hadn't written anything outside of my private journals for years. When it was my turn, I blathered for a while, unsure of how to describe my writing.

"I don't really write stories…" I began, "more like… I don't know. Life vignettes and descriptions, mostly in journals… a little stream of consciousness… but nothing, like, tangible I could publish."

My words drifted into nothingness, and whatever small semblance of confidence I had when walking into that creative writing classroom was deflated. My face felt hot as I realized how stupid I sounded. But my teacher was oblivious to my embarrassment as he looked at me cheerfully and said:

"Oh. So you're a poet!"

He said it like it was the most normal and pleasant thing in the world – like I wasn't straddling impossibly between genres, like I wasn't just some wannabe with hundreds of snippets of old writings scattered all over my bedroom floor. He hadn't seen a single piece of writing from me yet, yet he still spoke to me like I was a writer worthy of being in his class.

I will never forget how important that teacher made me feel. Don't underestimate the transformation that occurs when we can look at another person and choose to see them as the light of who they are – not the version of them that is insecure and hemming and hawing, not the person who is making excuses and living a much smaller life than we want them to. Learn to see the blistering light and potential behind someone's words.

In that teacher's writing workshop class, we had to write a ten-page fiction piece. On the day our story was due, we handed a printed copy of our story to each of our classmates, and by the next week's class they would read our story and return our manuscript with a typed page of feedback for the author. Then the class would spend 40 minutes discussing our piece in a workshop-type setting, treating our work as if it were any other piece of literature, posing questions to each other about plot and voice, and facilitating a lively discussion based on our words. The author would sit quietly and take notes.

It's nice to take a writing class. It's nice to talk about writing, to sit with other writers and discuss narrative and plot and language and the creative process. After so many years of keeping my writing under a bushel, it felt invigorating to spend time with other people who loved to write.

But the first piece I actually wrote for that class was the most tortuous ten pages I have ever written. I had no idea how much self-doubt lingered under the surface waiting to be tapped into until I was asked to write a fiction story that a classroom full of people would underline and highlight, argue about, debate, love, dislike.

I tried to write. And I tried to write. And I tried to think up brilliant story ideas and punchlines and characters, and I tried to fictionalize my own life, and I typed and hacked away. But the ideas wouldn't come, and when they did, they were laughable. My heart pounded with panic: *I'm not going to finish this…. I'm doomed… I'm not a writer… what was I thinking taking this class?* During a thirty-minute time block between my two jobs, I called my mom in hysterics from the floor of a random hallway of my college's law school building. *I can't do this. I can't write this.* I was breaking down. I was giving up.

I was breaking through.

Because despite my panic and fear and desire to feign illness and skip class, showing up to class empty-handed would be a far worse outcome than creating a ridiculous, plotless, what-was-she-even-thinking piece of writing. Nothing would be more embarrassing than admitting that I couldn't write one story. Nothing could further demonstrate defeat.

The night before my fiction story was due, I clunked out the words on my keyboard one after another, barely editing, praying that the words I needed were already fully formed somewhere out in the ether – that all I needed to do was to pluck them out of the air and get them onto the page. The night was peppered with stopping points where I froze in front of the screen, eyes bloodshot, overcome with a rush of belief that my writing was the worst anyone had ever seen.

But a deadline can be our most helpful master, especially when the assignment is due in 18 hours and we are fumbling for ideas, wishing we could just melt into the earth unnoticed for a few days. Constricted by a crucial deadline, we have little time for stopping points, tears, and Writer's Block. So that night I took a lot of deep breaths and momentary pauses, letting the fears rush through me, then looked back at my screen and continued to type.

I finished my piece the next morning, and I hardly glanced at it when it was done. I no longer cared whether or not it made sense. I stood at the library printer and watched the machine spit out twenty five copies of my story, sleepless yet secure in the knowingness that even if my classmates all hated my writing… I did it. I finished a piece of writing for the first time in years, and I basked in the feeling of that accomplishment. I felt like I was finally peeking out from behind my mask, birthing a story out of thin air, and sending it off into the wilderness to fend for itself. Like I was finally beginning to behave like a writer.

PART III
Resurrection

Share Before You Are Ready

When I was 21, my mentor and I created a farmer's market in the Rogers Park neighborhood of Chicago. We spent several years beforehand working together to make the market a reality, doing everything from hosting a faux farmer's market, to mailing out surveys to dozens of small Midwestern farmers, to establishing the perfect location and spending a day picking up urban litter from the job site.

On a peaceful Monday in June, our farmer's market launched with big white tents, blistering sunshine, and vendors asking us where to park their trucks. That first season, I co-managed the market and met some of the most amazing human beings I have ever known – strangers who started out as volunteers and ended up as family. I became hooked on the rush of creating something beautiful from scratch.

After that first season of the market came to an end,

it became clear that I wouldn't be involved in running it anymore. This wasn't by choice — it was the outcome of a basic fact: I was graduating from the university that was technically behind the entire project. It was time for new leaders to manage the farmer's market and shine. It was time for me to move on.

Part of me was peaceful about this. I trusted that the Universe was trying to nudge me into a new adventure, I adored the people who were going to manage the market, and I knew they would grow the market in ways that I hadn't even considered yet.

But I was also terrified. I was graduating college and had no idea when I would receive a paycheck again. I was sitting in Oprah's chair, feeling like the largest imposter on Planet Earth. My sweat and tears and identity and self-worth were all messily intertwined with the existence of this market, and now I was expected to smile, brush off my hands, and skip into my future without it.

And to top it all off, I was riddled with guilt over my secret dream to be a writer. My farmer's market had been a proxy for the bold, colorful, creative life I wanted, but without my farmer's market and without any credible reason to believe I had a future as a writer, I felt untethered.

The following summer, the farmer's market started its second season under new leadership while I sat on the sidelines. I eyed my future with a cold suspicion, believing I would never again create anything as beautiful as that farmer's market.

So in the middle of the night, at loose ends, with no idea where my life was headed, no big creative project where I could channel my energies, I finally started a blog.

Birth. Action. Death.

Neurotic Clinging.

Rebirth. Peace.

I am so fiercely proud of that girl who sat in her rickety office chair, propped her window open to ease the summer stickiness, and tooled around on WordPress for the first time. I am so proud of her first blog post where she admits, "I have no idea where this will take me," talking in circles about herself and her influences. I am so enamored with her willingness to begin. I am so grateful for her anger and her emptiness. After so many years of pushing her passion to the side, she was finally, *finally* a writer.

Take your dreams and start them now. Don't wait for someone to pluck you from the crowd and give you the permission, money, knowledge, or answers. There will always be a Realistic reason why you shouldn't begin. Begin anyways.

When one dream ends, another opportunity is waiting on the sidelines to swoosh in and fill the space. Part of me wanted to stay stuck in the fixation on my farmer's market forever. Part of me never wanted to move on. But I'm so glad I heeded the voice of the echo-chamber inside of me that didn't know where I was going, didn't know where the future led, yet still pleaded *Yes... yes... write... write.... start a blog.... begin...*

Be totally unreasonable. Admit that you have no idea where your efforts will lead. Cut through the mental static and confusion. Every single moment will be worth it. Bigger miracles will fill the void you thought you had. Share before you are ready.

If you want to write, start a blog. Don't wait until you

have the perfect URL, don't scratch your head thinking of the perfect name for your blog, don't read dozens of articles about search engine optimization and branding and staying on-message and acquiring readers. You can figure all of that out later. You will find your way.

Write little vignettes on social media. Create a magazine by hand and send copies of it to your friends. Find or create an open mic night nearby to perform your work. Create a weekly writer's group at your favorite local diner. E-mail a poem to a friend and ask what they think. Create a handwritten book of stories and give it to your grandparents to cherish. Take a writing class and make an effort to stay in touch with your classmates long after the class is over.

People are attracted to the glow of those who show up as their messy and authentic selves. Dive in today, just as you are, fully aware that you will learn and alter your strategy along the way. Your deepest and most fiery dreams will always, always be supported—all you have to do is make the first move.

"I Don't Know" is a Gateway

"I Don't Know" is the gateway, the Step 1, the launching pad for everything beautiful you will ever create. Unknowingness is part of the creative process and adventure – it's what sparks our divine curiosity and keeps us tingling and reaching at the end of our comfort zone.

"I Don't Know" is not the brick wall stopping us in our tracks unless we choose to see it that way. If we haven't done something before, of course we don't know exactly how to do it. But we must edge forward anyways, we must write badly, tinker along, learn as we go, and work our way through the muck.

There are all sorts of resources on honing your message, creating a brand for yourself as an author, and so on, but don't worry about that now. Focus on writing something down. Focus on trying a new style that you haven't tried before. Focus on getting your work out into the world for free. Focus on finding an organization of writers in your area and attending a meeting.

Start there and let the rest unfold. Later on, you can learn how to create a website and find a real editor and publish a book or write a book proposal. Later on you can learn about optimizing your website for clicks and creating catchy titles. All of those are valuable skills to pick up along the way. But start where you are.

So often I hear people say, "Well, my *dream* job would be to be a writer…" before rambling on about what kinds of books they would hypothetically write.

"Oh awesome! What kind of stuff do you write?" I ask in cafes and living rooms, at parties with strangers, in the doorway of yoga class. And more often than not, an uncomfortable silence follows. And then the dreaded words:

"Well, I mean, I don't really write that much. I haven't written anything in… like… years."

How are you going to have a career as a writer if you don't write? How exactly is an agent or publisher or reader supposed to discover you if you don't write? And even if they did discover you, even if you stumbled into someone on a street corner who could help you in your writing career, what finished pieces of writing would you be excited to show them?

This is, admittedly, the Tough Love School of Writing, and these questions don't evoke much joy and inspiration. But clarity is crucial if we want to get serious about pursuing our writing dreams, and in moments when we are floundering, procrastinating, and future-tripping, we can circle back to answering these concrete questions and keep ourselves moving forward.

I have been there. I was a college graduate sitting in Oprah's chair wondering how I had not become a writer yet, how my path had become so gnarled along the way. I wanted this big glamour moment; I wanted *Kelsey Is A Writer* blinking wildly on a marquee somewhere for people to smile at.

But I was waiting for Someday when I could finally begin. And Someday is a lie we tell in order to keep ourselves small and hidden. Someday will never present itself on a gilded platter. If you don't make writing a part of your life, then you won't create more writing, and your words will never be shared with all of the readers who could be touched and transformed by your message. After we tap into our dazzling childhood creativity and chip away at our doubt, we are left with just one task: to begin getting our work out into the world.

This is a tremendous time to be alive as a writer. We can write something and propel it into the world with a few taps of our fingers. We can play with our words on a screen, we can edit and jumble and delete and click them into place without having to erase out the smudges of typewriter ink. We can spend a few hours researching and emerge with the knowledge of how to self-publish a book or pitch an agent or find an online writing community or start a free blog. We can get instant feedback on our work, and if our friends and family don't like our writing, we can find a posse of people online who do.

I Don't Know is the key to starting every beautiful project of our lives. Hover in your unknowingness, but don't stay there; leap forward and trust your own ability to figure it out as you go. Forward momentum can be just the miracle you need to draw the right people, events, and synchronicities into your life.

Guilt, People Pleasing, and Dancing Monkeys

We have so many different and fascinating facets to our personality, so many personas and tendencies swirling around inside of us, and sometimes they come into contact with one another. I have a persona within me that I call the Dancing Monkey, and she is the queen of people pleasing. She is largely driven by guilt.

Her name is Dancing Monkey because she looks like the toy monkeys in cartoons that cheerfully clang cymbals together on the sidewalk for the pleasant strangers in pea coats who pass by and toss her a gold coin. Her function is to make everyone happy, to do as she is told, to never deviate from her fixed plastic perfection. She brightens moods, keeps everyone around her satisfied and comfortable, and receives compliments for her work, but she herself is in chains.

I know that I'm acting from that cramped-up space of the Dancing Monkey when I ignore my feelings about how I want to spend my time because there is one more social event to support, one more person I will disappoint if I don't see them immediately, one more obligation to say yes to. I am the Dancing Monkey when I make too many commitments and have to sweet-talk my way out something because of the pesky physical law that says my body can't be in two places at one time. I am the Dancing Monkey when I spend my entire birthday party pacing by the window, making sure I can greet every latecomer at the door, listening to my guests drink and laugh and chatter in the background without me.

And the moment I even consider writing, before I even pick up a pen, this people-pleasing Dancing Monkey in me starts to roar.

There are giant life events I still haven't written about, losses and reconstructions that I struggle to put into words because I question whether they are my stories to tell. When I'm in the Dancing Monkey mind zone, I lose track of what words want to come out because my brain has already launched ahead to who would be disappointed in me if I wrote that story, who would judge me, who would sue me, who would rip me to shreds. The guilt creeps around my wrists, silences my lips, threatens my aura with its invisible knives and daggers.

Our guilt does not help anybody. All our guilt does is hold us back, suck out our soul, poison our writing, and make us hollowed-out versions of the people we are capable of being. Our guilt keeps us small and obedient, clanging our brainless monkey cymbals together on command and wondering why we still don't feel free. We think we're helping the people around us by staying cramped and folded, we think they like us better because they can be more comfortable in our smallness.

But is it worth it? Is it worth it to zombie-walk and monkey-dance through a passionless life that someone else said we should have? Is it worth it to let guilt steer the direction of our writing?

Our guilt will not fix any giant social problems that are tugging on our heartstrings – the ones that we research and daydream about, the ones that make our stomachs churn and bring us to our knees. We need shimmering vibrant people to solve these kinds of societal problems, people who are willing to create full-on integrated lives that honor all parts of themselves. Even the creative parts. Even the not-so-glamorous parts. Even the Dancing Monkey parts.

When I sit down to write, I acknowledge the Dancing Monkey that clamors in my ear. She wants my attention. She wants to be seen. She wants me to be loved and approved of, and I want those things too. I let her rattle around for a while, but then I silently tell her to move on. I tell her that I'm writing right now and don't need her at the moment.

We must be unapologetic about breaking through the guilt, the "shoulds," and the expectations that have held us back. Our writing will crumble under the weight of everything we think we should do, and learning to unclench our grip on this guilt allows us to forge a path towards the creative life we have wanted all along.

Exercise: The Things Our Guilt Will Not Do

Guilt tends to creep under the surface, holding back our ability to write and putting a cap on how much joy and success we can achieve. A way to notice when guilt is running the show in your writing life is to think of all of the "shoulds" you hold yourself to. We can break guilt's chokehold by laying out our guilt-stricken thoughts and seeing them for what they are, empowering us to move past them and thrive as artists.

On a piece of paper, write out all the ways that guilt plays out in your writing life. Even if you clearly know that the story your guilt is telling is not true, write it down anyway:

I feel guilty that I am stressing out over my writing, while at the same time I walk by homeless people on the street every day who would be grateful to have this kind of problem. I feel guilty for wanting something more than what I have. I feel guilty that my family worked hard to allow me to be conventionally successful, and they will feel betrayed if I focus on my art.

When you're done, reframe and rewrite each statement by using the phrasing: ***This guilt will not_____.*** Try to keep these reframes laser-focused on the guilt itself:

This guilt will not help that homeless person. This guilt will not cure hunger, stop climate change, end war, or solve any other social problems. This guilt is just weighing me down. This guilt will not make me any older or any younger. This guilt will not empower me as a writer or allow me to share my words with the world.

When you're done, look at your new list of all the things your guilt will not accomplish for you. Keep this list close to your desk or writing workspace and flip back to it when you start to feel guilt creeping in, when you start to feel like you don't deserve to write with abandon.

Guilt itself can be difficult to distinguish – it often mixes and twirls with the effects of the guilt, making our triggers hard to pinpoint. By focusing on the guilt and everything that the guilt cannot do for us, we realize that it's safe to let the guilt go. We can finally start to break its shackles, writing not as Dancing Monkeys but as glowing and expansive beings with stories that are worth sharing.

Surrender

In writing, like in life, we can hustle as hard as we want.

I write whenever I possibly can, I have a hard-edged stance that Writers Block does not exist, and I feel startled when I'm not actively finishing and sharing blog posts. This action-oriented part of our brain is a key to our writing success because ultimately writing is an action verb; when we write, we are *doing*. We need to clang words together and see what emerges. We need to plow through our doubt and come up with some written words on the other side of that paralyzing emotion, even if those words aren't perfect.

But we must also remember the bigger, more effective power of learning to surrender.

We are tiny individualized pieces of a force energy that is so much bigger than us. Our writing is a reflection of this energy and this light, and our words spring up from this core of universal understanding. We don't need to "figure it out." We don't need to think our way into something brilliant or sexy to say, and as soon as we realize this, the pressure is entirely off. When we get into that zone of surrender, beyond our clinging and control and manipulation, we allow the full honesty and truth of our words to emerge. Writing is a process of letting go of every block that holds back our vivid self-expression.

You can try the alternate approach of attempting to carry the weight of your writing on your own shoulders. You can try to think your way through every solution. You can try to write one perfect word at a time until your sentence is drab and dry and wishy-washy and only half as vibrant as you wanted it to be. But don't you want to be astonished by your own words? Don't you want to be in such a creative flow that you don't know where these strings of ideas even came from?

What is it that you really want from your writing? Are you trying to write your way out of a day job? Are you trying to get someone to finally pay attention to you? Would you keep writing if you never published a single book in your life? If you never got paid for your work?

What if you wrote the most vivid and haunting piece that you are currently capable of writing... and only five people read it? Would you still be glad you created it? Or would you be fixated on the statistics and praise, hitting that refresh button neurotically, sinking into a lizard-like frozen-posed panic over why no one likes your writing? Are you losing sight of the magnetic force that brought you to creative writing in the first place?

The way that you declare and interact with the end goal of your writing will influence your writing practice at every step. There is no disconnection, no break in the action. If you're trying to write your way out of your profession, your writing will feel constricted because subconsciously you are fixated on money, book deals, dollar signs twinkling in your eyes, the fame that you never got but always wanted. Detaching from these outcomes of our writing life will give us the spaciousness to write freely in the present moment.

There is a deep and sorrowful resignation permeating our society, a foggy hypnosis where people find themselves identifying with ideas of lack and saying things like, "Well, you can't have everything," or "You'll find out soon enough what the world is really like."

This cynicism is the least useful attitude we can bring to our writing practice. If writing is what helps you access that joyful place in your soul, the world needs your writing – even if you never get paid for it, even if your words only ever circulate to the people nearest you. We have no time for you to pretend otherwise.

Postponing our dreams is the cruelest form of self-sabotage. Life is excruciatingly short, and plenty of moments are already frittered away; if we don't take the time now to do the things that make us happy, when else will we have the chance? Are you going to go to your grave with your books still harbored inside of you? When are you going to break free?

Surrender to the words that want to come out. Surrender to your writing voice, to the ideas that pop into your head, to the moments and characters of your life, to the urges that we don't consciously understand.

None of us know where this ship is headed. None of us know what tomorrow may bring, and none of us know why certain events in our past worked out the way they did. But the best action we can take is to step forward bravely in this moment, focus on the joy, and create a brand-new story.

Maybe we have squished our writing voices for decades, but we can choose to make today different, to crack out of our shell and fiercely dive into the tantalizing life experience we have always shied away from. We can surrender it all.

Fame and Letting Go of It

Once we are plugging along and finally writing, once we are working on our blog posts or poems or novels, our minds like to gallop ten thousand steps ahead of us and become fixated on tiny details pertaining to the future.

During my first year of blogging, I was living with my parents, two teenage sisters, two toddlers, and a pet frog. I wrote blog posts at night on my stomach on my sister's bed when I returned from my long workday commute, my time peppered by interruptions. At 7 AM the next morning, I would upload my heartfelt blog post from my parents' desktop computer in our kitchen and share it with my social media networks.

I would immediately leave for work, and I didn't have a smartphone at the time, so all day I wondered about the blog post I had written: *Did people love it? Did people read it? What did they say? Did they post any comments? Am I finally going to be discovered by a publisher?*

After all the twinkling of anticipation, I would rush back home and see how many people read my blog post… and I would be horrified to discover that only twenty people had read it. *Twenty people? All that work and soul-sharing for just twenty people?!*

Whatever excitement I built throughout the day was sucked out of me, and I wallowed in pitiful frustration that my audience was so tiny. Whenever I focused on how small my audience was, my dreams of growing my writing career would flatline.

If you tie your success to the quantity of people who pay attention to you, the payback will never be enough. There is no magic number that will ever satisfy you. You could be on magazine covers, you could be a bestselling author, you could move someone to tears and change someone's life, and still you would clamor for one more "like," one more admirer, one more compliment. The misery is from your frame of mind, the scarcity mentality of trying to hoard as many impressed people into your corner as you can so you can finally feel less alone. But that lens is distorted, and I was making myself miserable by seeing my readers through that distorted view.

The number of readers you have is not the truth of your being. The truth is that every single human being who clicks on your post has zillions of pulsating cells in their pointer finger that could have been doing many other things at that moment. Every person who "likes" your page, visits your website, uses their brain cells to read and process your work, tells you they love your writing, or buys your product, is a living breathing human being who has experienced ecstasy and loss, heartache and joy, grief and malaise and confusion. They are not just a Like. They are each infinitely holy, so let's stop agonizing in the false belief that we don't have enough of them.

Isn't it a miracle that we can share our writing with the world to begin with? Couldn't we have been born in all sorts of different time periods without libraries and the internet, without blogs and zines and social media, where we would have had to move heaven and earth to get into the elite club of published authors?

You don't get to decide whether or not the interviewer hires you. You don't get to decide whether or not your lover leaves you. And you don't get to decide how many people read your writing. You don't get to decide whether those people work in the publishing world or if they will swoon over your words. All you can do is show up, express your truth, stay in tune with the intention of service, and surrender the rest.

When we write from a selfish place of trying to impress someone, that energy permeates and dilutes our words. People want what you've got – they want your authentic voice, even if you can't always identify from your perspective what makes it so unique and special. The more I learn to let go of my attachment to the out-come and the more I remember that the numbers on my website statistics screen are not the measure of my writ-ing talent, the more miracles show up in my writing life. My boyfriend was at a party, and a girl I had never met told him, "Your girlfriend is the one with the blog, right? I read every single post." A coworker once stopped me in the hallway and thanked me for an insight they gleaned from an article I wrote months before. We can never fully know who is being impacted by our words, so the best we can do is let go of our attachment and trust that our work is being guided to the exact readers who need it.

Let go of the confines of what you think people want. It's time to go full blast, big-hearted, all-in. Your readers will find you. Your tribe will be drawn to your blinding flame. Your words will reach the people who need them the most.

Exercise: Launching Your Writing Into the World

Create a ritual, statement, poem, or prayer that you can use to center yourself into the energy of service whenever you launch your writing into the world. Let whatever you choose be an inspirational way to center yourself into the expression of love and service to your readers.

Maybe you want to create your own prayer, play your favorite song, or eat a celebratory ice cream sundae before you hit "Publish" on that blog post. Maybe you want to call your daughter or go for a walk or stare out the window and whisper "Thank You" before submitting your story to an agent.

Create your own ritual and use it every time you share your creative writing on social media, blogs, in e-mails to friends, or queries to agents and publishers.

Before I send my writing out into the world, I say a little prayer:

May this writing reach every single person who needs to read it. May their lives hum with the vibration of their own luminosity and greatness. May they shine. And may I let go of the outcome, knowing that everything in my life is working together perfectly for my highest good.

Feel free to use this prayer or write your own chant, prayer, or statement that works for you. A sense of ritual around publishing our writing not only centers us in the act of sharing, but also reminds us that it is a gift and a privilege to be able to find a writing audience – an honor that is worthy of reverence and gratitude.

Genre & Strategy

It is so tempting to get wrapped up in the strategy and how-to and publishing side of our writing: *What genre is this? Who is even going to read my work? How can I build an audience? I don't sound like any popular writers... maybe I should start trying to sound like them... wait, no, my voice is unique, right? ... Let's scroll the internet for several hours looking for answers....* This is one of our ego's favorite tricks because it diverts us from the task at hand: actually writing.

Once I started sharing my writing with the world, I got tripped caught up in trying to define what genre my writing fell into. I couldn't figure out how to describe my blog and writing style. I felt like I fell just outside the realm of self-help and spirituality because my writing wasn't very bullet-point "1-2-3-4-5 Ways to Happiness"-focused, but I didn't feel like I was literary enough to be considered a bona fide nonfiction writer either.

I developed a rambling string of words that fumbled out of me whenever people asked what my blog was about:

"Oh, my blog is like... self-helpy inspiration with a little poetry, I guess? But not too spiritual. But still real... like, based on my life."

(Awfully similar to my description of my writing in that very first college fiction class, and not exactly the riveting elevator speech that's going to motivate the masses to read my blog.)

I tussled with the "What *is* my blog about?" question for a while before finally surrendering to the understanding that I wasn't going to be able to figure out a definition on my own. Instead, I asked some of my most loyal and supportive readers what they perceived my blog to be about.

"You write about empowerment," one friend told me simply. I had never spent much time thinking about that word before or how it might describe my writing.

"You write about real-life stories in this really authentic way," another friend said, "and you talk about the tough stuff openly in a way that a lot of us are afraid to do."

I didn't know what value my writing provided to people until I asked them. Once I asked, not only did I feel clear about the contribution I was making to the world, but I was able to tailor my writing so it continued to embody what people already loved. Asking for help was scary; I felt awkward and self-conscious when I asked a few friends how they would describe my writing, and I braced myself to hear that they didn't actually like my writing at all. But more often than not, when you ask them, people are genuinely interested in helping your writing grow and providing the feedback you need to move forward.

Write now, share now, and let the genres and definitions follow you later. Once a piece of writing is complete, you may want to figure out what genre it falls into so that you can pitch it to the right audience. You will eventually need to compare your work to similar writers so that fans of those writers can find you. It sounds trivial and flippant to boil down your unique voice to a comparison with others, but there are thousands of readers out there who would love your work if only they knew about it. And one way they will find your work is, ultimately, through the authors and styles they already adore.

But those are nitty-gritty details to think about in the final stages of a writing project. In the meantime, don't let the fear of being genre-less stop you from writing in the first place. Your first flurries of readers will find you, they will adore your authentic voice, and they won't care what genre your writing falls into.

The Power of Community

Now that we're in the twenty-first century, with handheld pockets of vibrating fuzz that can tell us pretty much every answer we need to know, it's easy to operate in a vacuum. We can scroll through the photos and memories and enviable life of a friend-of-a-friend at a glance. We can see when the people we know are making big ripples in the world—writing books, creating projects, launching magazines, embarking on noble and charitable journeys. We no longer need to wait until the next high school reunion; we can see for ourselves that the people in our lives are creating some pretty powerful things.

It's easy to secretly admire their efforts in our own technological silence, keeping our findings and inspirations to ourselves. But every creator on this planet benefits from supportive and thriving communities, and communities can't blossom when we all operate in our own hunched-over glowy-eyed vacuum.

Inside of a microbrewery that I visited in New Mexico, a glass window separated the bar and taproom section of the building from the warehouse where they actually brewed the beer. Dozens and dozens of colorful bumper stickers were stuck on this window, and when I looked closer I saw that each of the stickers had a logo on it that represented another brewery from New Mexico or Colorado.

When I asked the bartender why a local brewery would have a public space to celebrate all of the other local breweries in the area ("Aren't they technically your competitors?"), he looked over at the bumper sticker window.

"Those other breweries? No way! If you're visiting us, be sure to visit them too. If they succeed, we succeed."

Writing works the same way. Other writers aren't your competition – there are plenty of stories, readers, money, and publishing opportunities to go around. If someone finds the work of one of your writer friends or idols, they will be more easily able to find your work too if you all share one another's work freely and without nervousness or envy. So help each other out.

When I started the farmer's market, the people I loved moved heaven and earth to shop there that first year. My friends and family members changed their work schedules, biked during heat waves, and took wildly frustrating combinations of buses and trains to be part of my specific farmer's market. It didn't matter that most of these people already had access to larger and more popular farmer's markets that were located much closer to where they lived.

They showed up. They showed up not because it was

convenient for them, but because they wanted to support me and my project.

And since then, I have learned to pay it forward. When my friend opened up a local tea shop, I drove to Detroit a few weeks later, braving two flat tires and a snowstorm, so I could check it out. When my minister wrote a book, I bought three copies immediately – one for me and two to give away. I didn't even know what the book was about or if any of my friends would like it. I just knew that I wanted to spread the word and be part of his success because his inspiring words had changed my life so greatly.

This is how we create a more collaborative, intimate, relationship-based world. This is how our communities weave together and thrive. We don't question whether or not our friend's comedy show will strike a chord with our sense of humor – we shut up and buy our tickets. We don't idly scroll past the facebook post that says our friend needs to coach a few people as part of a life-coaching certification – we sign up for a coaching session immediately. We show up for the people around us in the knowingness that our own projects will also be fully, effortlessly supported.

During the process of writing this book, I had all sorts of doubts about whether I was smart enough, talented enough, interesting enough, or good enough to write the book that I wanted to write. I doubted it would be useful to anyone. I thought it would be too generic, too sugary, too obviously self-published that anyone who wasn't already my friend would stay far away.

But I knew that my book would be supported by the people who are already part of my world. I knew that my friends, ministers, acquaintances, teachers, and coworkers would step up to the plate and read it, share it, and buy it for their friends. I knew that it would make its way into the hands of every person on the planet who needs it.

And that's because I have spent so much of my energy celebrating and supporting the projects of the people I love. When you build friends and a community and a life, and when you choose to show up for them in whatever way you can, they will show up for you too. When our writing lives start to feel frustrating or hopeless, when we feel alone, when we have moments of questioning where our talents lie, let that be a call for us to give a little more of our time to our friends and family who are spearheading other creative projects, writing-related or not.

Supporting others lifts us out of our misery, so shop at their small businesses, buy their art as gifts, and share their writing with everyone you know – even if it's in the same genre as yours. All of your goodwill will come rushing back to you at a later time. When they succeed, you succeed too.

Exercise: Micro-Sharing

Find a friend or writing partner who will hold you accountable. Let them know that this exercise is not the moment for them to be nice, mushy-gushy, or bend the rules in your favor. All they need to do is stick to the rules.

You are going to write a three-page piece of creative writing on the topic of what you ate for dinner last night. (Or what you didn't eat. Or what thoughts pulsated through your head that day, where you were, what you were thinking about.) Single-spaced, double-spaced, hand-scrawled, whatever.

There are no more stringent rules than that, except: You must give it to this person in exactly a week. If this friend is also a writer, the exercise can go both ways and after a week, you must both exchange your three-page pieces of writing with one another.

Talk to this person to make sure you're both clear on the deadline and on how you plan to share your writing with them. Do whatever it takes to get your work to this person in the allotted timeslot. They are waiting for it, it is disrespectful of their participation in this exercise to give it to them late, and if you don't turn it in, they will call you and remind you and hold you accountable.

This kind of exercise can feel jarring – not as squishy and compassionate as the go-at-your-own-pace kind of creative process. But there is a time for creative meandering, and there is a time for aggressively meeting deadlines. Honor yourself enough to believe that you are the kind of writer who *finishes* things, and sometimes that means we need a strict deadline to make the leap, carve out the time, and get it done. Try this mindset on for size and see what feelings, fears, and excuses arise.

Hacking Away

After I had been writing in my blog for a few years, I traveled to New Mexico by myself with my laptop over my shoulder and the intention that I was going to hunker down and write my first book, or at least part of it.

Somewhere between drinking habanero fudge lattes, buying painted tin trinkets and knockoff turquoise jewelry, breathing chilly adobe air, and daydreaming about what it would be like to live there, I managed to write 15,000 words on that trip. But I had a difficult time getting any words to flow, and when it came to writing a book I ran straight into a giant writing block I didn't realize I had:

I'm not capable of writing a book… certainly not one that would be cohesive and helpful and remotely intelligent. My attention span is so small and flittering that I can't even sit still for a two-hour movie. What am I doing? What am I thinking?

No matter how far along we are in our writing careers, the same doubts will continue to surface. Our fears will take different shapes than they did before, and as we break victoriously through one fear, we will turn around and find that same fear confronting us in a new way. Writing is a process. Pushing through our own self-doubt will be the biggest obstacle between us and our writing for as long as we choose to write, and it is a battle worth fighting over and over again.

Those first 15,000 words of my book were painful to write. They felt robotic, like a third grade book report that hovers on the surface of what needs to be said and tells every boring detail of the story, word for excruciating word. The vision of the book in my mind was so beautiful, so glowing and colorful and inspiring, and I couldn't reconcile that vision with the plodding words that were coming out of me.

When I think of the writing process, the image that first comes to mind is of a giant abandoned lot, overgrown with enormous thickets of bushes and gnarled plants. Something beautiful is nestled in the middle of these bushes, but the act of getting to it is overwhelming; the enormity of the task sends you into a paralyzed panic, and you realize you have no idea where to begin. So you work for hours, hacking away at these bushes so you can get to the treasure inside of them, sweaty and clueless and covered in burrs.

Then when you step back to admire your valiant progress, you discover that the whole scene looks exactly the same as it did when you started. Despite your efforts, there are still impossible bushes everywhere, with only minor hints that your labor has made any impact. You are nowhere near the center of those bushes. You have so, so far to go.

And you stand still for a moment and you want to cry hot tears of exhaustion, but instead you take a deep and determined breath. You know, infuriatingly, that those bushes won't disappear without your effort. All you can do is keep going: hack by hack, bush by bush, word by word.

The hope is that eventually something awe-inspiring will emerge beneath all those bushes—a clearing, an eclectic purple house, the book you are trying to write, whatever you originally wanted to discover. Something you couldn't have possibly found without chopping away as you did, something you couldn't even discern at the beginning but that ends up being more magical than you could have imagined. Something that in the end makes you take your eyes off the page and think, *Did I really write that?*

As writers, we have to trust this process. If we stop as soon as we're frustrated, we will never accomplish what we set out to do. Instead of writing a book, we will take one look at those dark bushes and hide instead. We will let our dreams fade, we will walk away and assure ourselves that there was nothing behind that thicket anyways – that we shouldn't waste our time on such silly things. We fail to realize that if we stick with our writing project long enough, we will develop a knack for breaking through those initially uninspired strings of words.

Writing is gritty. Writing involves sullying our hands in the stickiness of our subconscious, where we can't see what's behind those bushes and we don't know how our efforts will weave together into a cohesive whole. But we have to start somewhere.

If a writing idea appears in our minds, it comes equipped with all of the means and knowledge that we need to write it. We may need to grow into our confidence as writers before we can work on it, we may need to mull the idea over and take stabs at it from different angles, we may need to do some research, but at no point in time are we given an idea that is too big for us. It isn't possible. We are bigger than our most radiant and exciting writing ideas, and we are capable of bringing them all to life.

We may not think we know how to publish our own book, hack away at a storyline, write from a different character's perspective, or share the true rendition of what happened, but once the idea is planted, once we are inspired and transfixed by the pull of creating our stories, we don't need to figure everything out by ourselves. We can trust that the guidance we need is on its way. We will find the people, the words, and the information we need to get our work out into the world. There is no other way.

Pretend it's a blog post, I kept telling myself in New Mexico, inhaling and exhaling and trying to edge my way through those first fledgling words of my book. *Pretend it's a letter to Mom. If you can't write a book, you can at least write that. One word at a time.*

I took a deep breath and kept slicing at those bushes—a sentence here, a snippet there, a note to write about a specific memory in a spot that already seemed too full. I let my first hazy over-generalized sentences lead me towards what I was really trying to say, and then I deleted them once I filled in the blanks. I trusted that I would be dazzled by the finished product, even while questioning how I was going to pull this off.

I breathed into that sunny horizon, felt my angel wings thumping and expanding between my shoulder blades, stretched my fingers against the desk, and kept hacking away.

Exercise: Publishing and Abundance

Walk into a bookstore. Let yourself become still and centered and take it all in—not in the rush of shopping or trying to hunt down that one book you want, but stand at the entrance of the store for a moment and absorb the scene around you. Breathe the papery air. Feel the little inky letters in every single book make their way into your bones.

Slowly, consciously, like a moving meditation, walk through the bookstore. Point to individual books as you go along, either physically or silently, and affirm:

That person published a book.

And that person published a book.

And that person. And that person. And that person....

Think about each book as you point to it: There is

a living breathing person on the other side of that book, a person who is not much different from you. And they created a book that is now nestled calmly on a bookstore shelf.

Everything you want is within your reach. You are surrounded by physical proof that thousands and thousands of people publish books every year. Most of those people have agents. All of them have publishers. Many of them have gone on book tours. These books got the sacred *yes* that you are looking for. Most of these people once daydreamed about writing a book, much like you are right now.

Let hope and possibility fill your spirit as you keep walking. Think about all the smiles and book launch parties and contracts and hugs that resulted from all of these thousands of authors writing and publishing their books.

And that person got published.

And that person achieved their dreams.

And that person probably wondered whether or not writing was even worth it.

And I bet that person has an agent.

And that person was probably so close to giving up at one point.

And a publisher said yes to that person... and that person... and that person....

All of this was possible for every single author of every single book you see, and all of it is possible for you.

Your ego may try to sneak in and derail this exercise by making up its own stories: *Most of these people are already famous... I doubt all of these people actually wrote their own books... Compared to the number of rejected books every year, this is still a small number of books in the grand scheme of things.* Mindfully observe those thoughts as they arrive, and then let each one keep rolling past. You know by now that those thoughts are not the truth of your writing life.

You are trying to program your subconscious mind to realize that all sorts of unknown people are getting published in the present moment, that all sorts of agents and publishers and readers are working hard to find you.

Don't leave the bookstore until your heart feels full, brimming with the knowingness that a book is within your reach. Carry this feeling within you when you write, and conjure it up when you start doubting your own abilities. Repeat as often as necessary.

Where Publication Meets Service

Art for art's sake is sacred and beautiful. Getting words onto the page at all is a miracle, and writing just for ourselves is holy; we can be whoever we want to be. We can be catty, we can be heartfelt, or we can be dramatic and angry and explorative. We can nurture our hidden soupy parts and nudge ourselves into being a little more imaginative, a little more genuine, a little more direct.

We can write happily and privately for the rest of our lives if we wish. But if we chose to share our writing, new questions emerge, rooted at the core question of: *Why am I sharing this with the world?*

There is no correct answer to that question, and each writer will have a mishmash of ever-changing responses. But getting clarity on the purpose behind our writing, whatever that purpose is, will keep us anchored to the essence of what we want to bring forth.

A holy boldness emerges when we share the nitty-gritty details of our lives. We don't truly understand the experiences of anyone else on this planet, so we can't write their stories for them– our sparks of truth lie in our daily experiences, our goofy revelations that are so universal yet so personal. I tell stories about my life all the time, as do my favorite friends and writers, and when they tell their stories I am drawn in.

But where is the divide between self-absorbed and self-expressive? What makes us pick up one memoir and feel like the author is speaking directly to us, while we can't even finish reading another book because the author sounds too self-important?

Before I put any of my writing out into the world, before I publish a blog post or put something on social media, my universal question is: "Is this helpful?"

Will someone feel inspired, heard, or supported by reading it? Will I make them laugh or nod their heads with recognition? Will my fiction story distract them from the realities of life for a brief moment? Is my writing a beautiful piece of art that I want to share, which is helpful in its own right? Is there anything of value to others here?

If the answer is not a resounding "Yes!" to one of these questions, I don't publish the piece. If my answer begins and ends with, "Well, you know, people will get to see a snapshot of my life and my feelings and stuff…," then I don't publish the piece.

Sometimes I edit that piece until it feels more help-ful and relatable to the audience I'm trying to serve.

Sometimes I leave the words alone for a while and let them soak in each other's energy as I sleep, as I work, as I move through my day. And one day, months later, I will find that original piece of writing when I'm fumbling for something to write about. I will dust off its narcissism, cut out the self-important parts, and tie it back to a bigger truth that transcends my life. I will douse my writing in the energy of service in hopes that someone will read it and nod in recognition of the universal anxieties we share.

Is your writing helpful? Or do you write to coddle yourself and fish for compliments?

Is there a faint possibility that someone out there is struggling with the same self-doubts as you are, and they might see this piece and be comforted by our universal human experience? Or are you just sharing this to inflate your ego?

Is your project going to transform someone's life? How? Why? Why not? What is your driving force? Pursue these ideas. Let them crawl into your bones and find their own answers.

These questions aren't meant to breed self-criticism. This exercise isn't about second-guessing yourself or keeping all of your writing hidden because you don't think they will help anyone. It's about becoming conscious of what you're bringing forth into the world. It's about becoming more of who you want to be, and witnessing every uncomfortable writing tendency that pulls your efforts off-kilter.

We create for ourselves, to piece together the kaleidoscope of our crystallized individual experience on Planet Earth, but creation is an act of service too. Our world is flawed enough by the cruel conversations we hear on the train, by the hate crimes, by the poverty, by the economic systems that leave swaths of humanity in ruins. We don't need to add our voices to the pettiness and mediocrity and dysfunction. We need to be brave enough to create something that matters.

Own your truth. Acknowledge the intrinsic power of your life. Talk about your joys and your devastations and your blunders and your miracles. Make art from them. Channel your experiences into your spectacular vision. Talk about the ideas and books and places and people that lift your fog.

Learn how to navigate this wild, sometimes-ruthless, often-astonishing world of ours—then share what you know. Show us your life. Tell us about the lessons you haven't learned yet, the ones you're still reaching for in every fumbling conversation, every wince of self-criticism, every outburst of anger, every fiery need to be right.

We're trying to learn those lessons too, so be our courageous teacher. Peel back the layers until we shake with recognition of our common molten human core, our blazing divinity that we can't always see.

Doubt yourself sometimes. Wonder if you're being too narcissistic.

But always, always, stay anchored in that energy of service. Let it gush through your conversations and carry you to the people that crave your big-hearted expression.

Be Willing to Change Directions

When it comes to writing, there is no grand linear summit to climb. There is no gold medal at the end, no point at which we fold up our tents and declare that we are finished.

I'm a nice Capricorn girl; I want my writing process to be a steady, one-step-at-a-time process that clearly leads to the top of a mountain. No deviating paths. No 4 AM panics over my worth as a human being when I write something horrible. No instances of pouring weeks of my life into a piece of writing before realizing that it doesn't reflect my true voice at all. No realizations that I must hopelessly start over. No wasted time.

Writing is a humbling practice; it circles back in jerks and starts, reviving our creativity and uniqueness on some days, reflecting back our bitterness and perceived limitations on others. Sometimes we need to spend days working on a piece before we realize that one tiny detail, maybe a sliver of something in our journal, is what we were drawn to write about all along, and everything we worked on until that point was just a warm-up. Sometimes we figure out that the story we wanted to share really isn't as funny as we thought it was. Sometimes we need to pull back from a piece we're working on because the words are just not gelling.

When I started writing my book in New Mexico, I told everyone I knew that I was writing a book. I put my declaration on the internet, in my blog posts and social media blurbs, to both hold myself accountable and generate excitement. I created an extremely tight deadline for myself with a detailed schedule of when I needed to write each chapter. The book was going to be a self-help book, reminding readers that they're not broken and that they have much to offer to the world. I hadn't solidified what made my book any different than any other self-help book, but my plan was to start writing it and figure out the rest later. I was also planning on self-publishing the book, which meant I had a tremendously steep learning curve ahead of figuring out the publishing industry on my own.

I wrote tens of thousands of words – on trains and airplanes, on lunch breaks, in my bedroom at 3 AM before my eyelids would finally sink shut. But the more I wrote, the more the words of the book felt fruitless and stale. Every chapter fell flat, and no matter how much soul I tried to pump into it, the words still looked like spineless inspirational quotes on a page. I felt like I was one more inauthentic plastic doll who smiled and told people to live their best lives, gritting my teeth so hard that my jaw gnawed together and my blood vessels popped.

The last thing I wanted to do was change directions. I had a deadline. I had people asking how to pre-order my self-help book. And I wanted to be the kind of writer who followed through on a book project, who had something papery and tangible to hold at the end of this process. I was tired of flittering around, starting to write books but never finishing them, as I had been doing for several years.

But the intuitive feeling that my self-help book manuscript was off-key would not subside. I asked the Universe for signs, and I received them in the form of wild nightmares and a foreboding tarot reading from a friend. My thoughts switched to panicky desperation: *Is it better to write a bad book than write no book at all? Or will a bad book hurt my name and career?*

The grisly doubt-ridden process of writing that self-help book opened floodgates of inspiration within me in other ways. The more frustrated I got with my book, the more insight I gained into how messy and imperfect the writing process can be. I avoided writing my book, and instead I spent more time blogging about my disjointed writing process. I noticed I was inspired to write about writing – I loved being a divine writing cheerleader, I loved imploring my readers to keep writing, to break through doubt, to try all sorts of exercises that had helped me as a writer.

One serene afternoon, I had a moment of clarity on my commute home from work. *You know what would feel amazing?* I thought as my train rolled into my station. *Not writing this book.*

So I stopped. I took a few days off from writing, and I didn't tell anyone about my plan to ditch the book; I wanted to let my emotions compost into one another for a few days. And then I decided to push back the deadline, ignore the hundreds of hours and 40,000 words I had written, and write an entirely different inspirational book about the writing process... which ended up being this book.

I had to meander around for three years writing on my blog to understand what I actually enjoyed writing about. I had to write half of a generic self-help book to realize that I really just wanted to write a book about writing all along. Each of those steps was absolutely critical to my artistic unfolding. There is no such thing as wasted time.

Follow the energy of where your writing is taking you. Sometimes we are just creatively blocked, and in those moments it's our responsibility to move through those blocks to reveal the beautiful writing underneath. But when our hearts are completely detached from our work, it may be because we're being called to create something larger and more luminous than we previously knew we were capable of.

Writing is not a race; there are no winners, there are no losers, and there are no trophies at the end for writing a bad book by an arbitrary deadline you set. Listen to your inner guidance enough to realize when it is time for you to change direction.

Giving Ourselves Permission

You deserve to take up space. You deserve to inconvenience others every now and then.

So much of our writing journey is about giving ourselves permission to speak, to share, to write beautiful things and mediocre things and question whether we have any talent at all (hint: we do). Every time we edge out onto the page, every time we seek out opportunities to share our work, we flex our vulnerability muscles and remember what it feels like to be truly seen and acknowledged.

And we must also give ourselves permission to live the life of our dreams.

Not just the checkbox-checkbox-checkbox-accomplishment-checkbox-checkbox little dreams we achieve here and there. Those little dreams are beautiful—the trip you always wanted to take, the apartment of your own, the short story you submitted to a magazine.

But what happens when those dreams start to feel small? What happens when your passions don't feel so big and tantalizing anymore? What about your own expansion?

When was the last time you gave yourself permission to do what you *love* with your life?

Not just what you like. Not just what you can live with. Not just the half-hearted tasks you know you can perform in exchange for a paycheck. Not just what is reasonable. Not just what you think your parents or grandparents or boyfriend will love.

What you *love*.

Let's say you want to write a book. Don't just give yourself permission to write a crappy book, a book that no one reads, a book that you expect to be mediocre, hastily pulled together, and thoroughly unlovable. Don't tell yourself, "Hey, at least I will have written a book!" Don't fool yourself into thinking that you will feel satisfied if you write a lukewarm, vanilla book that doesn't ignite any interest in the people who read it.

Crack through the doubt. Crack through the upper limits that you have given yourself. Toy with the idea that you are capable of writing something that people will cherish and adore.

And then throw your whole heart into it.

People need what you've got, and when you hold back, you withhold from them the opportunity to laugh and grow, to tune into the world your novels could create, to nod and weep at the honesty of what your words express. You don't need to be any more qualified than you already are. You don't need published books, letters after your name, or legions of fans. You've already had your heart broken, you already don't know when you're going to die, you already know what it feels like to slither down and sink into confusion. You are qualified. You are a Writer. You just need to begin.

If a dream doesn't feel big and expansive anymore, let it go. A new dream is on its way that is more bold and colorful than anything you have created thus far. A new adventure is hovering around the corner, waiting for you to tune in and say yes to its call. You are powerful beyond measure. You can do anything you want. When we listen to the callings and messages that our life is trying to reveal to us, when we discern what truly brings us joy, we can be the luminescent versions of ourselves that we were meant to be all along. We can finally be free.

Freewrite: Where Have You Sold Yourself Out?

Freewrite for ten minutes on the question of how you have been holding yourself back.

Where have you been hiding, lying, or lingering on the sidelines? Where have you sold yourself out? Who have you been pretending to be? And what are you going to do about it now that you know this?

Don't Put On the Brakes

So you've hit a moment in your life when everything is falling into place.

You landed the writing opportunity you've been manifesting. You emerged from confusion and found your voice, your posse, your Life Purpose, and a few long-lost notes from middle school to guide you on your way. You're feeling giggly and sparkly. You smile a little more, you pace around the hallways a little less, you write in notebooks and share your work with the world. You used to spend time pondering just how terrible your words were, and now you spend that time unabashedly creating even more words.

Stop for a second. Honor where you are—pause in the wonder and awe of it all. How did you even get here? Didn't you used to be terrified to write?

Deep bow of gratitude for everything you have accomplished.

Now keep going.

When things are going well, it can be tempting to stop asking for more. "I finally made it!" we declare, hoping to wisely sip our ginger tea and look back at our lives from a mountaintop at the end of the journey.

But what happens when a new opportunity pops up? Will you approach it with the same gusto you once had? Or will you inch away from it, content with the new life you've made, mumbling, "That would be unreasonable, I don't have the time… or money… I don't know how… I'm happy with the way things are."

Don't those thoughts sound a lot like the doubtful thoughts that plagued us when we first started writing and sharing our work?

As we expand, our dreams and possibilities expand, and the sparkling wild achievements of the past become a part of our norm. The blog we launched becomes the blog we forget about. The book we wrote becomes the first book that we wrote, way back when, before we learned so much and wrote so many more books.

Our new situation in life becomes our new comfort zone, no matter how far we have come. Just The Way Things Are becomes the new bubble we cling to. When Life is going really well, commit to expanding yourself further rather than retreating back into who you were. Let the floodgates open wide.

Creativity is cyclical and infinite, so this isn't the end of your unfolding. When we're centered in gratitude, we can access the kind of unlimited thinking that otherwise feels forced and mechanical. We get to daydream about our future and actually believe it. We get to see how far we can stretch our vision.

When life is going great, keep asking for more. Write that novel you always suspected you had in you. Take that trip to Costa Rica that your family is hesitant about. Ask your boss if you can move to the New York office – unabashedly, willing to be brave and resilient in the face of a No.

Keep yearning. Keep stretching.

We still have a lot to transform in this world: a lot of books that haven't been written yet, a lot of kindness to dole out, a lot of unhappy people who need shoulders and yoga mats to cry on. We need you to stay awake, to cut through the muck and have those difficult conversations and stretch your spirit further than you thought was possible.

Dozens of undiscovered dreams lie dormant in you. New challenges await you that you don't yet realize you're prepared to meet. As more abundance flows in, you will

make different choices about how to spend your time—
*Do I hire help? Do I make this change so I can reach more
people?*—and those choices will expand your impact
even further.

Just don't go on autopilot. Don't get too comfortable.

Revive your hunger. Be insatiable.

Your successes so far are just a glimmer of your successes to come.

And you still have some stretching to do.

You Are Needed

I helped plan a retreat at my university that guided students to explore their vocation: the special gifts and talents we have all been given and how they fit into this wide
and swimming organism of a world.

The retreat planning team focused on four guiding
questions, and we created inspirational speeches and activities for each question:

"What brings me joy?"

"What am I good at?"

"Where does love fit in?" and

"What does the world need me to do?"

These are tremendously profound questions to journal
on, meditate on, stick on our mirrors and ponder while
we brush our teeth. I love these questions. I ask them of
myself whenever I feel stuck.

But our group was divided over the "What does the
world need me to do?" question. I saw the question as
an invitation to plunge into the energy of service, to per-
petually keep the principle of non-harmfulness front and
center in our actions. I didn't think it had anything to

do with picking our passions based on what the outside world might want at a given time, as that would deviate us entirely away from our own callings and joy.

Several other people saw the question differently, and they used a story to illustrate their viewpoint. The story they told goes like this, in my words:

You could find great joy in being a shepherd, herding sheep could make you incredibly happy, and you could be really great at it – meeting the requirements of the first three questions posed. You could love being a shepherd with a passion springing from somewhere deep and graceful in your bones, and your shepherding of sheep would satisfy those first three questions of vocation.

But it's the 21st century, and the techno-savvy Western world does not need shepherds in the 21st century. Shepherding would not fit into the question of "What does the world need me to do?" so it's up to you to find another vocation that is more suited to the urgent needs of the current world. If you love shepherding, you had better pick some other calling because the world doesn't need another shepherd right now.

I hope this story helped someone grow in their personal development, and I hope it focused someone's clarity, but this story didn't work for me.

I believe that when we start thinking this way, we poison ourselves with Dream Guilt. We start weeding out our dreams and telling ourselves logical reasons why we shouldn't go after them, and if we keep at it, we may look back on our lives one day drenched with regret and debilitating unhappiness, all because we didn't think the world needed what we have to offer.

What if Angelina Jolie had said in the 1990s, "Well, the world doesn't need one more actress, so never mind. I'll go get a nice little job in business or something." She may have been correct by conventional thinking: actresses come and go, fame flickers, someone else would have starred in her roles. But would the world be the same? Would her humanitarian impact still resonate around the globe, would she inspire people like me who want to burst forward and live bold lives despite personal struggles? Or is it possible that the world *does* need people who are willing to crack themselves open and follow their hearts and talents, no matter how shadowy the trail, matter how many naysayers tell them their work is frivolous and unnecessary?

Our self-doubt, our fear, and our ego will already give us myriad reasons why we shouldn't follow our dreams. Our inner voice clamors somewhere in our chest, but we already struggle to hear its dampered sound through the gnawing trivialities of day-to-day living.

Add those self-sabotaging tendencies to Society's spindly finger demanding that we stay in line, and add in some well-meaning-yet-fear-laden advice from our family and friends... this is a recipe for disaster, forcing us to stay meek and obedient and quiet. Surely we don't need to add one more layer to the mix by scolding ourselves and saying that the world doesn't need our gifts and callings.

The world needs you to do whatever lights your heart on fire. No more, no less. Your burning desires have been placed in your heart for a reason, and you owe it to yourself to follow their nudges wherever they lead. Your path will change. Your love will grow. Your spirit will soar. Your opportunities will open up. Your smile will radiate so blindingly that your bathroom mirror will barely recognize you.

Of course a sense of service should be integral in our actions, and of course we should never stop helping, never stop learning, and never stop educating ourselves on the social problems that impact our world. But the world needs us most when we're fully committed to our life and our passions – not when we go through the motions of doing something we don't want to do, all the while yearning for another path.

The world needs so many things, and we can't always see how our individual callings fit into the whole, but let's muster up the faith that they do. In a grand cosmic twist, I discovered that O'Hare Airport in Chicago recently decided to use sheep and goats to graze on grass on the airport property. And do you know what position they sent out a job posting for?

You guessed it: a shepherd. As it turns out, if your joy and calling—and, yes, your vocation—is to be a shepherd, the 21st century needs you after all.

Let It Be

Let it be easy.

The people who love you don't love you because of your writing. They love you because you are You. Remember that core glowing truth when you start overthinking your creative process.

You have a big life, full of color and light, zigzags and backroads, smiles and gratitude and coffee and shouting and frustrated tears dripping onto your shirt. Your writing is one glowing and important piece of that life... but it's still just a single piece.

In some moments, we must mobilize our inner strength and choose to break through. We avoid our writing, we deny our creativity, and we let our voice slip away... until we don't. Until we choose to set our jaw and sit in that chair and write and claw and bleed and express despite the doubts and apathy and inner questioning. Heavy on the willpower. Triumphant with success.

In other moments, we must step away from our inner motivational speaker. We must wander. We must rest. We must softly focus on the littleness of our lives, stare at mulch while our kids climb on pine-green monkey bars, and embrace each moment for the strange miracle that it is.

Let it be fun.

Let your writing be simple. You have nothing to fix. You have nothing to improve. You have no reason to drive yourself into a deranged panic over which adjective to use.

Relax.

Let go of the expectation that you must share your deepest and most scarring sorrows through your writing. Maybe those are the stories you want to tell – maybe you want the catharsis of release, the swelling of support, the illumination of how far you have come in the face of what has happened to you.

Or maybe those are the exact stories that you don't want to tell. Maybe you will write about everything except for your deepest traumas and bone-chilling regrets. Neither approach is better than the other. This is not a competition. You cannot win or lose at writing. You can write about whatever you want.

You have stories to share. You have a distinct audience, a sliver of the whole that cares deeply about your work – even if they haven't found you yet. They want your perspective. They want to read your writing. And the moment you start sharing your writing openly and freely, without expectation of receiving money or fame or respect in return, that audience will eagerly make their way towards you. They will wonder where you had been hiding for all of this time. They will want more.

When you start to quiver with doubt, when you start to question whether you have any ounce of zest and soul and creativity left inside to share: concentrate on that audience, fixate on their needs and desires, and write something for them.

Write whatever you need to hear. Let it enfold you. Let it become your life. Let it be your imprint on the people who adore you the most.

Let it all come rushing out.

Shine

If writing ignites your heart, work it into your daily life and stop coming up with reasons why you don't have the time. Start creating things now. Make art on your train ride home. Don't wait for the world to give you permission and ample amounts of time.

And when you feel the flutterings in your heart encouraging you to share your work, even if you don't feel ready… share it anyway. Let us soak in your wisdom and creativity. Let us laugh with your characters and shake our heads in disbelief that someone out there can describe the universal complexities of life so clearly that it feels as if they are reading our minds.

You are doing a disservice to the people on this planet if you withhold your brilliance and talent from us. Your words could transform us, make us think about something in a new way, change our minds, save our lives, and break us open. How dare you keep them cloistered away? How dare you brush them off and carry on like you never wanted to write anyway?

If you really dive into your writing, your life will never be the same. You will live on the edge of your comfort zone, rocking, teetering, and brave. Your non-writing life will seem bolder and less grey because your courageousness will bleed through to every area of your life. You will stand a little taller. You will say, "No thanks, I need to write tonight," and mean it. You will churn out words of inspiration and find your friends, your heroes, your calling.

We can't keep our writing lives separate and isolated from the rest of our lives, even if we try. It isn't possible. It all starts to run together into a life experience that becomes more bold and luminous and soulful every moment.

I once sat in Oprah's chair with a quivering plastic smile, feeling like a fraud, realizing that I had shoved my writing passion to the side and built an inauthentic life in its place. Since then, my life has been totally transformed. I'm still working in the sustainability industry by day, coordinating environmental programs from my cubicle (which is decked out in crystals, a vision board, and fluttering positive quotes stuck on notepads).

But now my attitude is completely different. I love my

sustainability job, and the people at my workplace know me as a writer, not as someone who fakes her way through life and hides her creative dreams away from others. My coworkers ask about my writing, they follow my blog, and they offer to throw book launch parties to celebrate my success. My life expanded exponentially the moment I decided to take myself seriously as a writer within the confines of my existing career.

Maybe my career trajectory will change over time and veer more towards writing, and maybe it won't. And either outcome is completely okay because there is no more guilt bogging me down. I can sit confidently and know that no matter what my diploma or business cards say, I am exactly where I need to be. The gift of self-acceptance I have found through writing has revived my internal fire and reminded me that I can do anything I want with this evolving, multi-passionate, beautiful life of mine.

One of my very first blog posts was a poetic explanation of why I write – that blog post ultimately evolved into the "I Write Because" exercise in this book. Soon after I wrote it, my sixth grade English teacher asked if he could incorporate that blog post into a first-day-of-school activity for his students. To say I was honored would be a tremendous understatement. Since then he has used my writing in his class every year, and dozens of students have pored over my words, discussed what it means to be a writer, and written their own pieces based on mine – all from a simple blog post that I originally scribbled in a spiral notebook.

I've been asked to teach writing workshops despite no formal training. I get to stand in front of a classroom of fidgety teenage girls and ask, "So who here is creative?" and watch every unsure hand stay glued to the desks. I get to witness the transformation at the end of our time together when a few girls shyly start to admit that they are creative after all. Tiny revolutions. Some of the greatest miracles of my life. These are the liberating moments that are possible when we dare to start showing up in the world as true and bona fide Writers.

And I have two nephews who are five years old—little blonde twins who write their own books at the kitchen table, who daydream of robot coconut trees, and who still think they can do, be, and have anything in the world. I want them to hold onto that feeling of hope and possibility for as long as they can. I want to bottle up their unapologetic creativity and sprinkle it onto the hearts of every self-doubting writer on this planet.

I have all sorts of other young people in my life, sisters and cousins and friends, and each one is trying to find their unique place in this world. I wanted to write and publish my first book as a testament to their creative potential, as an exercise in being the role model I want to be, as a nod and a prayer that demonstrates we can truly create anything we want. We can be the fire starters. We can be the rabble rousers. We can be the writers.

I wish you the best. I wish you tears of half-madness, sparks of inspiration, bravery and crazy faith. I wish you the perseverance to leave your phone in the other room, to turn off the internet, to stay centered in your creative zone, to begin. I wish you the knowingness that you don't need to Figure Anything Out, the reminder that you are just the faucet, the vessel, the crystal through which divine creative light comes rushing through.

You are electric, you are talented, and you are on fire with a spark of holy aliveness that no one else can replicate.

Every word you have ever written, in journals and on greasy napkins and flowery notepads, has propelled the evolution of the Universe.

You are not as alone as you think you are.

You are here to express the truth of your life. You are here to share that truth with the world.

You are here to transform the planet. You are right where you need to be.

And now is your time to shine.

A Prayer for Writers

May you remember that there is no perfect word
just like there is no perfect boyfriend, no perfect eyelash,
no perfect way you should have responded to the cruelty
spewing from a friend's grieving lips at the high school
lunch table
so many years ago.
May you fuss and fret and
stew in your perfectionism,
call your mom in hysterics in the middle of the night,
and choose to forge ahead.
May you let go.
(Perfection is a cruel dirty myth.)
May you find your voice in flickers and starts,
in the fumblings and breakthroughs and hope that unleash
generations of stories, retellings, flipped perceptions,
fierce expressions.
May you fall in love with Kerouac or Atwood or Bradbury
when you're fifteen years old and dredging your way
through adolescence –

may you spend years imitating your influences, letting them swirl their way into your words
until you can no longer tell
Which is Who and What is When
and Who you even are anymore.
May you accumulate piles of journals whose raw wisdom guides you home,
and may you honor the power of your Voice
that glimmers through the cracks of those long-ago scribblings.
May you know that there are no Good Writers or Bad Writers –
just Writers that Write and Writers that Say They Write.
(Pick your camp wisely. Avoid the sidelines.)
May you skip a few social outings and delve into some
painful memories and make a few writer friends along the way.
May you explode with excitement every once in a while
in awe of the words that come out,
cooing and admiring them and brimming with pride.
May you know the miracle of saying "I made that."
May you anchor in the glowing seed of your heart that
one writer's success is every writer's success. Be gracious.
(Jealousy is a cruel dirty trap)
May you believe in the magic of sloppy first drafts –
may you give yourself permission to write them,
may they reveal the embryonic mush of the words
that rattle in your bones and whisper for release.
May you never stay small.
May you serve the world boldly, vividly, in such a fiery craze that you forget about

looking good
impressing your parents
being reasonable
finding an agent
getting famous.
May you remember that you are just a channel for a dazzling force
so much bigger than you can comprehend.
May you ignore the advice of the times.
May you smile with teeth.
May you shine.

Radiant Recommended Reading

The books below have completely transformed the course of my writing life. If you're looking for a place to continue developing your writing wisdom, start here. Read these books. Soak them in. Let them lead you to more books, more writers, more inspiration to light your creative path:

Bird by Bird: Some Instructions on Writing and Life — Anne Lamott

Writing Down the Bones: Freeing the Writer Within — Natalie Goldberg

Zen in the Art of Writing: Essays on Creativity — Ray Bradbury

Juicy Pens, Thirsty Paper: Gifting the World with Your Words and Stories, and Creating the Time and Energy to Actually Do It — SARK

Spread the Light

Word of mouth, person to person, heart to heart is still the most effective and soulful way of spreading inspiration. If you enjoyed *Robot Coconut Trees*, please consider leaving an online review, buying a copy for a friend, blogging about it, or taking some other action to share its light with other writers.

And let's keep in touch! I would love to hear about your writing stumblings and successes – here are some places where we can connect online:

Visit my blog at KelseyHorton.com
Find me on Facebook: facebook.com/kelseynic
Tweet with me: @kelseynic
Share the Instagram love: @kelseynichorton

Acknowledgements

To everyone who has participated in my writing journey: Thank you. You know who you are. You sent me e-mails full of publishing tips the moment I declared I was going to write this book. You shared my blog posts. You edited my words and pointed out the moments when I deviated from my true voice. You became closer friends with me than we already were. You cheered me on. You let me read your first drafts so we could evolve as writers together. Thank you for every single moment. I will always be in your corner.

To the beta readers who made the energy of this book shine: Celi Barragan, Jillie Johnston, Stephanie Pearson, and Adam Schmitt.

To the editor who made the words of this book shine: Kathleen Marusak.

To the designer who brought this book to life: Damonza.

To my family: Thank you for teaching me about Beatniks, saving my blog posts on your hard drives, molding me into the woman I am today, and believing in my literary ambitions from the very beginning. We are an amazing group of imaginative rock stars, and I am so grateful for each one of you.

To Mark Reed: Thank you for saying yes to being part of this luminous, wild, who-knows-where-we'll-end-up life journey with me.

To Bodhi Spiritual Center and Unity in Naperville: My spiritual homes. Thank you for holding me up and urging me to fly.

To MEEA: The family that I didn't know I needed. Thank you for everything.

About the Author

AT AGE 9, Kelsey Horton had her first piece of writing published in a children's fashion magazine. She was supposed to write an article about sunglasses, but the message of her article was that readers would look dazzling if they wore whatever sunglasses they loved most. Her writing style (and fashion advice) hasn't changed since.

Between then and now, Kelsey has volunteered with refugee resettlement initiatives, created a farmer's market in Chicago, and participated in sustainable agriculture projects in the US and Panama. After neglecting her creative dreams for years, Kelsey started her blog, KelseyHorton.com, that has helped thousands of readers around the world break through stuckness and write their hearts out.

Outside of her writing life, Kelsey is a yoga teacher, Reiki practitioner, aunt, sister, tree hugger, and travel enthusiast. She talks with her hands, wears colorful clothes, and still smiles in awe every time a stranger reads her writing.

Made in the USA
San Bernardino, CA
19 December 2016